POLITICAL TRANSFORMATIONS OF THE CONGO

Political Transformations of the Congo

Dr Mbow M. Amphas

The Pentland Press
Edinburgh – Cambridge – Durham – USA

© Dr Mbow M. Amphas, 2000
First published in 2000 by
The Pentland Press Ltd
1 Hutton Close
South Church
Bishop Auckland
Durham

Typeset by Carnegie Publishing, Carnegie House,
Chatsworth Road, Lancaster
Printed in Great Britain
by Bookcraft (Bath) Ltd, Midsomer Norton

*To my daughter Achtas and
all children of her generation*

Contents

List of Tables and Maps

Tables:

Maps:

Acknowledgements

IN WRITING THIS BOOK I have been assisted by a number of people in a number of ways. I am particularly grateful to my friend Dr Jennifer Jarman for reading the manuscript, and to students of East and West African Seminar for their continued interest in my work. I would like to thank Susan Drucker-Brown of the African Studies centre of the University of Cambridge for encouraging me to publish a book on the Congo to contribute to the area of African Affairs, especially French-speaking Africa. The Department of Social and Political Science of the University of Cambridge was helpful in offering me its encouragement and cooperation.

I thank Matilde Viannello for her friendship and understanding during the crucial two years in which the manuscript was written.

I am grateful to my publisher, Rachel Gowling, for her guidance in preparing this book for publication, and especially to Adelise Annie for her constant support and for freeing me from many of the tasks of everyday life.

Abbreviations

AEC   Association des étudiants Congolais
ANP   Assemble Nationale Populaire
APN   Armée Populaire Nationale
CC   Central committee
CGT   Confédération générale des Travailleurs
CMP   Comité Milataire du parti
CNR   Conseil National de la Révolution
CSC   Confédération Syndicale Congolaise
EMSR   Etat Major Spécial Révolutionaire
IMF   International Monetary Fund
JMNR   Jeunesse du MNR
M-22   Mouvement du 22 février
MNR   Mouvement National de la Révolution
MSA   Mouvement Socialiste Africain
OAU   Organization of African Unity
PCT   Parti Congolais du Travail
OCF   Office Congolais des Forêts
OCMC   Office Congolais des Matériaux de construction
PCT   Parti Congolais du Travail
PPC   Parti Progressiste Congolais
SIAN   Société Industrielle et Agricole du Congo
Socome Société Congolaise de meuble
SUco   Sucre du Congo
UAIC   Unité d'afforestation du Congo
UDDIA   Union Démocratique pour la défense des interêts Africains
UGEEC   Union générale des étudiants et éléves Congolais
UJC   Union de la jeunesse Congolaise
UJSC   Union de la jeunesse socialiste Congolaise
URFC   Union Révolutionnaire des Femmes Congolaise

Preface

THERE IS NOTHING more exciting than to analyse the Congo's turbulent history. Since Independence in 1960, the country has undergone radical changes with tenacity and courage. The trade union, which was the vehicle of the revolution in 1963, urged mass participation and vigilance against 'Imperialism'. The policies of nationalization were adopted, giving the state control of the economy. The building of the Congo's one-party system in 1969, focused on 'Scientific Socialism', followed by the 'Anti-Imperialist' struggle. For this reason, the Russians and the Chinese saw the Congo as a sound base for spreading revolution in sub-Saharan Africa.

Now, because of continuing economic difficulties, the Congo is open to the West and has adopted the I.M.F.'s structural adjustment programme. Another chapter is being written in the Congo's political history. Thus it can be asked: Has pragmatism won out over ideology? Has the Congo turned back on Marxist ideology? Which road is the country following?

As circumstances have changed, so should strategy. The purpose of this book is to show how the Congo can turn its failures into successes. Obviously, the challenge of the coming years will be the success of self-sufficiency in food and abundant jobs. There is no doubt that the drive towards Congo's political, economic and social success is in the hands of those who understand that 'Marxism-Leninism' is not as it was yesterday, and dogmatism is not up to date. The key to success for the coming years is interdependence and openness. The time has come for the Congo to be open to the West, to South-East Asian countries and international institutions.

As the book deals with the political history of the country, it is impossible to avoid identifying the names of those who were the political children of the period of independence, or those who are the product of a 26-year reign of revolution that has shaped the way the Congo is today.

This work intends to provide the reader with an understanding of the Congo's political, economic and social transformation from independence to the present. A historical perspective has been adopted in this study, because policies have been different in different periods since independence.

xiii

Immediately after independence the Congo focused on reconstruction, and then from mid-1963 to 1968 it stressed the Socialist road in the hope of promoting growth. From 1969 to 1977, the Congolese Labour party (P.C.T.) was torn by quarrels among its leaders and by 'a systematic purge'. Since 1979, however, the Congo has succeeded in maintaining an unusual degree of stability, despite the ever-present threats of ideological and tribal factionalism within the ruling party, and despite economic pressures.

The book is divided into five parts. Part I presents a full understanding of current political developments. All recent political problems can be traced to the colonial inheritance.

Part II discusses political change from independence to the present. It stresses how the power moved from a 'neo-colonialism régime' to the 'revolutionary one'. It describes also how the country moved from a 'civilian régime' to the eruption of the military in the political scene. This part is based entirely on secondary material and documentary sources and lays no claim whatsoever to original research. As much of the material handled in this part is historical in nature, I have relied a great deal on books, theses and articles for information. One thing is certain: in interpreting these sources, I have been guided by my own view and, in particular, a coherent framework of understanding that seeks to make sense of the specific features of the Congo's political change.

Part III is based on direct familiarity with the country as well as study and research involving Congo. This part focuses on the military coup in July 1968, which ended the reign of the 'civilian régime'. The book shows that what happened in July was the military and civilian Marxist response to the stifling of the revolution. However, the military committee's interference in the political scene in 1977 was seen as a military dictatorship, while in 1979, Nguesso's arrival as President was seen as a return to orthodoxy. It was a clear indication of the ascendancy, not only of civilians over the military, but also of the militants over the moderates.

Part IV deals with the major constraints on Congolese economic performance. The book identifies four major bottlenecks: low productivity in the agricultural sector, lack of capital, poor management skills and the results of the oil failure. This part also deals with the bases for economic progress. For example, it is well known that the Congo has a lot of natural resources, small population and educated workers.

Part V discusses the prospects of the country. The book analyses how the Congo can accelerate growth, how it can create more jobs, how it can achieve self-sufficiency in food.

The conclusion is an optimistic one. 'There is still hope' – provided we learn from failures. The rule is that when circumstances change, so should strategy.

Cambridge, 1989

INTRODUCTION:

A Look at an 'Exceptional Socialism'

FROM INDEPENDENCE ON 15 August 1960 to the present, the Republic of the Congo, formerly Middle Congo (Moyen Congo) and recently the People's Republic of the Congo, has undertaken many social, economic and political transformations which make its history fascinating in itself. A useful way to understand what is happening now in the Congo is to refer to the past.

Since the birth of the nation, five Presidents have run the country. Apart from their will to lead the country towards prosperity, tribal tensions still remain the big problem. Traditional beliefs are still strong, often existing side by side with the political aspects. Among the main ethnic groups are the Vili on the coast, the Kongo centred on Brazzaville and the Teke, M'bochi and Sangha of the plateaux in the centre and north of the country.

Historically speaking, the Congo has moved from reactionary policy to Socialism with Massamba-Debat, and to Scientific Socialism with Ngouabi. After Ngouabi's assassination, Yhombi Opango, his cousin, took over power. After no more than two years he was accused of not following the road to Marxist-Leninism and of encouraging corruption Because of these shortcomings, he handed over power to Sassou Nguesso, who had for a long time been the closest friend of Ngouabi. He restored Marxist-Leninism, which had been shelved for two years.

There may be relative political stability, yet the economy stagnates. Careful steps should be taken to restore the vitality of the economy. Since oil production dropped, hit by the fall of the dollar, the government has had to renounce implementing some of its planned objectives (1982–1986). There is no choice: the Congo has joined the queue of countries relying on the I.M.F. (International Monetary Fund). Thus a programme of austerity which requires the slimming of the public sector, to put more money into productive ventures – especially agriculture – and to contain the heavy external debt burden, has been adopted. [1]

Even if the Congolese leaders are preoccupied with building Socialism, they cannot only depend on the Soviet Union and Cuba, which provide the government's rhetoric, and train and equip the Congo's armed forces.

The other side of the problem is the need to ensure the economy has renewed cooperation between the Congo and the West, especially France, which is the Congo's largest economic trading partner. As we will see later, this cooperation with Western countries has been a good thing in itself, even if some inequalities still remain.

Compared to other countries of Africa, the Congo is regarded as one of the more developed countries. It does not face drought or flood, which are the causes of starvation. In addition, its population is 1,922,429 according to the census of 1985; an average density of 5.6 per square km, low compared to óther African countries. Natural resources are abundant and include crude petroleum, natural gas, gold and zinc. Yet the revitalisation of the Congolese economy has not happened. The central problem – the lack of management – reflects that.

Several members of the Congolese Labour Party, at least at the beginning, have been appointed to the state enterprises, not by merit or competence, but by ideological criteria. A few non-members, who have the skill and the know-how, are occasionally appointed. There is nothing surprising in this, as the Party is the centre of power. Nevertheless, when Ngouabi was dissatisfied with the performance of the members of Party, he pointed out that only hard- working, efficient and serious workers would be appointed. No longer would he tolerate those who put their own interest above the people's interest. [2]

The course of events for the Congo was extremely tortuous. A long time ago, the Congo, through its leaders, theoretically declared war on sabotage and corruption, capitalist behaviour, laxity and irresponsibility among managerial personnel; but in practice little has been done. There is a wide gap between rhetoric and reality. If, by chance, you go to the Congo, what catches the eye is the contradiction between slogans which call the young, women and workers to vigilance against Western imperialism, and Brazzaville's shops, which are glittering treasure troves of luxury goods, most of them imported directly from France. [3]

This reflects the day-to-day, month-by-month, development of policy in the Congo. More significant is that the Congo's aid from the capitalist countries remains the highest relative to its gross national product (G.N.P.), of any Francophile country and aid from this source continues to be of major importance. [4] This aid does not compromise Russian influence or degree of influence in the Congo. As far as we know there are many who have been trained in Moscow in the Congo's armed forces as well as in the Party. [5]

It seems clear that neither the emergence of a revolutionary régime following the failure of Fulbert Youlou, nor the improvement of the revolution by the introduction of 'Scientific Socialism' has affected the relationships between Western capitalist countries and Congo.[6]

In this respect what has occurred in the Congo is particular in itself. It is equally instructive if stress is placed on how the radical rhetoric does not prevent the Congo depending on France. More realistic and pragmatic than Guinea or Mauritania, Congo has had the wisdom to remain in the French zone. Despite many years of 'Scientific Socialism', the Congo retains an untrammelled private sector. Is it a paradox?

Why is there still Western investment in the Congo? How does the Party justify the path it has chosen? Is there a contradiction between, on the one hand, Congo's ideological militancy and vehemently radical rhetoric and, on the other hand, the country's continuing dependence on Western aid? How to combine ideology and pragmatism? Is there any hope for the country, in spite of the economic collapse? This is certainly a good reason to study this contradiction, which brought social and political transformations in the Congo. Soon, as we can see, Congo's experience could be an example for hardline Marxist countries like Angola or Mozambique.

In the study of the Congo's social, economic and political transformations, special attention will be devoted to policies adopted by each government since independence in order to achieve general welfare. Beginning with the 'neo-colonialist' regime of Youlou Fulbert, the history of the Congo has been influenced by the history of the tribes and their political leaders. While the second stage was the creation of the new 'Socialist régime' throughout the last months of 1969, radical policies predominated alternatively with the creation of the Party and emergence of the military at the direction of the state. There will be a time for drawing conclusions later on; but first a look at an 'exceptional socialism' in the Congo, in which I examine the reasons that lead the Congo to openness. So far Marxist ideology survives and still remains an official ideology. It is obvious that economic difficulties take the Congo in two directions at once: Socialism and Pragmatism.

As it has been practised in the past, Scientific Socialism should have left the country fairly poor. Now I suggest that the best solution to build up socialism is to combine Marxism and pragmatism. To accept the Western countries' presence, learn from them and co-operate with them, will benefit the Congo.

Notes

1. Le Monde, 27 Août 1985, 'Le Congo s'éfforce de redresser une situation économique alarmante'.

2. Marien Ngouabi: 'Vers la construction d'une societé socialiste en Afrique.' *Présence Africaine*, (Paris 1975, p. 222).

3. See an interesting article of Jon Swain: 'Parisian chic rivals Marxist rhetoric in people's republic'. *Stirn* (March 1, 1981).

4. The Congo. Africa South of the Sahara 1987, Sixteenth Edition (Europa Publications Ltd. 1986, England).

5. Le Monde, 22 Avril 1987, 'La révolution Congolaise tiraillée entre Moscou et le F.M.I.'

6. Le Figaro, 29 Janvier 1979, 'Congo: Un socialisme Africain pas comme les autres'.

Preliminary Understanding of Current Political Developments

INDEPENDENCE WAS THE PRODUCT of subtle negotiation between the colonial power and those who were going to represent its interest. This negotiation has determined the course of the modem history and political developments of Congo. It has been said that the Congo before independence had a population of 600,000. No sizeable town existed. Brazzaville, a capital of Congo, was regarded as an administrative small market town. Pointe-Noire was a built-up area of some thousand inhabitants, the city dwellers being 1.7% of the whole population. The rest of the population were essentially farmers. Little by little, the Congo has become an urban community. [1]

What explained the rapid urbanization of the Congo was not the success of slave economy, but an exceptional place occupied by the Congo among countries belonging to French Equatorial Africa (Afrique Equatoriale Francaise – A.E.F.) [2] created in 1910.

Throughout most of the colonial period, the Congo shared its history with three other African territories in the Federation of French Equatorial Africa. It is worth noting that the four territories – Middle Congo, Gabon, Oubanqui Chari (now the Central African Republic), and Chad – were jointly administered from the Federation's headquarters in Brazzaville. Observers underlined that France had encouraged an individual role for the four countries: stock breeding was the speciality of Chad, farming was the characteristic of Oubanqui Chari, Gabon was involved in timber, while the Congo was the centre of civil administration. [3]

Congo has continued this tradition by encouraging the training of civil servants instead of favouring the agricultural sector. As a result agricultural output has declined with farmers turning away from the rural areas to the cities, generating a continuing rise in unemployment. It has been noted that neither Socialism, introduced by Massamba-Debat, nor Scientific Socialism, by Ngouabi, did much in order to tackle an unemployment problem which was our heritage left by the neo-colonialism régime of Youlou Fulbert.

In addition, an increasing relative population which rose from 969,000 in 1960 to 1,811,000 in 1986 cannot be fed by a rural population who are still using traditional methods. To feed its population, the Congo has to import food at a high cost, which has only proved possible thanks to revenues derived primarily from exports of wood, potash and oil. [4]

Although nothing of political significance emerged from independence and after, there was no doubt that the most important success achieved by the Congo was to send children to school and to allocate grants and scholarships to all students. The government devotes 15% of its operating budget to education. [5] This percentage is going up. The Congo is one of the leaders in Africa in educational terms. This has been explained by the country's unusually high rate of urbanization and Brazzaville's importance to the French.

Too Much Empty Talk but not Enough Work

After independence the Congo moved very quickly from the 'neo-colonialist' régime to Socialism in its two aspects: Socialism Bantu with Massamba-Debat and 'Scientific Socialism' with Ngouabi. Whatever the form of Socialism, the Congo is facing a contradiction between the theoretical appeal of Marxist-Leninist ideology and the practical realities of economic development. It is true that the members of the Party were more eager to make speeches than to increase production.

At the beginning of the revolution, people spent a lot of time attending political meetings instead of working enough. As a result the economy was slowing down. [6]

Before the Congo took over 'La société villegrain', the output was 100,000 tonnes of sugar, but in 1976 the production of sugar cane had declined from 100,000 tonnes to 30,000 tonnes. As a result the Congo was obliged to import sugar from West Germany. In Owando, a Ngouabi native village and that of his cousin Yhombi-Opango, the production of palm oil has declined. People worked only two hours a day, [7] instead of the usual seven hours.

It came as no surprise when Marien Ngouabi, Chairman of the Party's Central Committee, said in one of his speeches, 'State enterprises have been adding to the budgetary deficit we inherited from the past. The fault is not with the enterprises, but with the lack of managerial experience ...'. [8]

At the same time the Party called on its members to apply the principle adopted by the Fourth Trades Union Congress, 'He who does not work neither shall be paid'. (Qui n'a pas travaille n'a pas droit au salaire.) Often, the government's objectives were expressed in terms of Marxist-Leninist principles; but these principles were not implemented. As there were contradictions between ideology and economic realities, pragmatism emerged as a force which influenced policies.

The Emergence of Pragmatism

In 1963, there was no doubt that Socialism was regarded as the inevitable way for the Congo to overcome its economic difficulties. Congolese workers were encouraged to take part in revolution. Capitalist exploitation was strongly denounced. Pro-Chinese leaders took control of the economy. At the same time, relations were reinforced between the Congo and Eastern countries. France became the most dangerous enemy. [9]

By 1981 the Congo had taken the step towards opening up to West-European countries. A young, dynamic and wise Congolese President realized that the 'Congolese Socialism' would be successful on the basis of pragmatism. Nguesso claims to be a devout Marxist, but it is clear he places national economic self-interest above ideology. First economy, then ideology. This new approach should deserve more attention.

Neither the Russians nor the Chinese provide substantial aid to the Congo to help it to reach a solution to its economic difficulties. Needless to say, France is by far the most important supplier of aid, and is the major trading partner and business partner in extraction of petroleum. Also, France is the eighteenth customer of the Congo (2.8% of exports). The United States of America is the second largest customer of the Congo's petroleum. The South African Republic buys 5% of wood exported by the Congo. [10]

An Italian company works one of the smaller petroleum deposits, and US companies are interested in prospecting.

What cannot be forgotten are the economic reasons that lead the Congo to co-operate with the Western countries. A young Congolese diplomat, quite drunk, was haranguing a member of the Russian Embassy staff, banging his fist down on the table, 'You Russians overrate yourselves; you think you still influence events here; but let me tell you, Monsieur, Soviet Communism in Brazzaville is dead. I, for one, prefer to have the French here than the Russians any day'. [11] Soviet Communism is not truly dead in the Congo. Of course, there are those who fully appreciate the significance of the October Socialist Revolution and the changes it brought about in all the continents.

Why is the Congo still Marxist?

The basis of legitimacy in the Congo is related to the doctrine of Marxist-Leninism. To be appointed as head of a public enterprise, ambassador, or a member of Cabinet, it is important to be revolutionary. One other factor is that after one hundred years of anti-colonial struggle, only experienced leaders with ability to organize masses can run the country. In such circumstances no one can compromise his function by neglecting Marxism, which confers legitimacy on the Congolese leaders. The denunciation of Imperialism is regarded as a means of empathising with people's misery.

French-speaking states have been exploited by France. To put an end to the exploitation, young Congolese intellectuals have adopted Marxism. Subsequently, all public services, transport systems and foreign companies were nationalized and more government control introduced throughout the economy.

At the stage of the National, Democratic and People's Revolution (Révolution Nationale Démocratique et Populaire) the Congolese Labour Party, 'has as its priority aim economic independence', to be followed in the next stage by socialization of the basic means of production in the People's Republic of Congo'.[12] The stage of national, democratic and people's revolution has been defined by the Extraordinary Congress of the Party in December 1972. The revolution is national since the Congo continues the struggle for national liberation, against foreign, chiefly French, capitalist domination. It is a democratic revolution since in the cause of this struggle the Congo is mobilizing the people, the vast majority of the working people of town and country. The revolution is the people's revolution because the Congo has decided to advance to Socialism.[13]

Drawing on its struggle against Imperialism, the Congolese Labour Party has absolutely the right to refuse to allow the non-members of the Party to run the country. However, behind the anti-imperialist struggle one has the impression that the Party has put its own interest above the people's interest.

Who is to Blame? Imperialism or the Members of the Party?

It is too easy to blame Imperialism for all the difficulties. If we go into details, it is possible to assert that we can share the responsibilities. True, the Congo has always been a peripheral region of the world capitalist system:

it has inherited a heavy burden. [14] Congolese authorities have reacted to this colonial past, and have undertaken to shift the colonial structure. [15]

In the same way, Hugues Bertrand had described the claims of the Congo for foreign capital, principally French, in 1975 in the following manner: 'a country destined to ensure the majority of activities of a staging post for capital in the customs union'. On the one hand services, both technical and financial, are much better developed there than elsewhere. Numerous small metal working shops and various services begin to function, while almost half the credits destined for the customs union are delivered to the Congo,

On the other hand too, transit activities rapidly expand, necessitating the enlargement of the port of Pointe-Noire, the increase of the carrying capacity of the railway and the river fleet on the Congo and the Ubanqui. Comilog (Compagnie Minière de l'Ogoué) is starting the construction of a railroad connecting Southern Gabon (region of Franceville) to the Congo-Ocean line to evacuate manganese. Finally a number of small and medium-sized industries produce (for markets of the customs union) cigarettes, beer etc ... or even the entire community sugar. [16]

Besides the situation described above, it should be noticed that the new generation of leaders of the Congo has not run the country well. A patrimony left by the French has been destroyed. While there used to be a lot of facilities to travel from Brazzaville to Bangui before independence, today the road conditions are deteriorating. [17] Worse still, 'la declaration du 12 Decembre 1975' of the Central Committee of the Congolese Labour Party has denounced smuggling practices in the state enterprises and a plethora of manpower. Administrators, decision-makers and trade-union representatives have been accused of recruiting workers on the basis of establishing a custom. [18]

It is said that during the French administration's period there was no corruption. Now corrupt behaviour and public scandals are increasing. Illicit earnings often exceed the official salary by two or three times.

CHAPTER I

The Building of the State

What is the nature of the State in the Congo? And what does the concept of State mean? So far, scholars continue arguments about the nature of the State in Africa. Some of them talk about the Primitive or Traditional State, while others defend the idea of a Feudal State. [19]

The important question to ask is what the relationship is between African societies and the general evolution of humanity. It is known that Marxists have distinguished primitive community, slave society, feudal society, capitalist society and Communist society. It is very difficult to say in the context of Africa whether the State was slave, feudal or not There was certainly a form of feudalism which was different from European feudalism.

Perhaps the most important issue facing many African countries today, of course beside the debt crisis, is the weakness of the State, which is not able to lead the country to development. Much is the fault of the State.

Neo-Colonialism's State

Colonization cannot be seen in terms of civilizing indigenous people. According to Gonidec, there is a relationship between socio-economic transformations of European countries and colonial expansion. [20] Even if colonization was determined by economic interest, one can also say it was related to other factors. Karl Marx had already pointed out in the case of India in 1853, the double mission of England: one destructive, the other regenerating. He added, 'the Indians will not reap the fruits of the new elements of society scattered among them by the British bourgeoisie, till in Great Britain itself the now ruling class shall have been supplanted by the industrial proletariat, or till the Hindus themselves shall have grown strong enough to throw off the English yoke altogether.' [21]

Colonial rules have influenced African countries, from cultural and religious domination to political structures. When most African countries became independent in 1960, their élites, trained and educated at colonial schools, perpetuated the structure left by the French or English rule. So, what we often call neo-colonialism is the extension of colonial powers in Africa, largely represented by Africa's leaders themselves. In Archie Marfeje's eyes, a distinction needs to be made between colonialism, which was an unmitigated imposition, and neo-colonialism, which is a contractual relationship even if accompanied by very severe constraints.

Independent governments can contract into or out of certain arrangements. In East and Central Africa we have the contrasting example of Kenya and Tanzania, and Malawi and Zambia.[22] Whatever this difference, one can safely say that neo-colonialism is seen as a perpetuation of a prior situation. African countries usually recruited civil servants on the basis of metropolitan examinations. In most of those countries, after independence, the French factor in the administrative structures still remained quite significant.

Colonialism may be over, but its moral and cultural effects still remain. Ngouabi once observed that real independence is still to be achieved. Most of the African countries are still economically, politically and culturally dependent. The State structures the colonialists had created to suppress the masses continue to stand and many of the conditions needed for progress are lacking.[23]

Is the State Proletarian or Capitalist?

For many in the new states of Africa the greatest disappointment of post-independence has been the question of the nature of the State. It would be a mistake to ask whether the African State is proletarian or capitalist. These categories don't reflect the African reality. What can be stated is the fact that African countries offer us a new type of State, which according to the circumstances could support either a Marxist or a capitalist regime. That is the significance of the new State. What is true for other countries of Africa is also true for the Congo.

In African contemporary history, two things – the state bourgeoisie and the business bourgeoisie – were profoundly influential. Sometimes, these two groups found it necessary to collaborate in order to get rid of the colonialism; sometimes they found themselves in conflict. Mali, between 1960 and 1968, was the classic example of this.[24]

It is generally accepted that colonisation was the main cause of the emergence of local bureaucrats. In Congo, for instance?, French administration had contributed to the creation of the group of administrators needed. The nature of State can appear clearly in the light of this evolution. Bureaucratic bourgeoisie which includes military, administrative and traders, run the country in accordance with their own profit interests and not with those of the genuine development of that country itself. This is to say, in the Congo, that the State is an instrument of a bureaucratic class. Lenin has argued that the purpose of the State is to establish a public order which will serve the interests of the minority, not those of the majority. [25]

What Lenin taught in the young Soviet Republic is still relevant today. It is the bureaucratic bourgeoisie which uses the State for its own interest. To some extent, this group is exploiting the rural masses as in the colonial period.

The Bureaucratic Bourgeoisie and the Workers

The bureaucratic bourgeoisie as a class is often considered very difficult to define by its position in the economic structure, as it does not possess the means of production. It remains a class only by the fact that it is conscious of itself as such, and always views its own interests as opposed to those of other groups. It is an intermediate group between workers and owners of the means of production.

From a Marxist perspective, the representatives of bureaucracy are considered as a reactionary group. Almost everywhere people belonging to the bureaucracy live in good conditions, holding high status and filling technical positions. Does this bureaucracy exist in the Congo? There is no doubt that those who handle administration and the state sector of the economy are the élite who represent the aspirations of the bureaucratic bourgeoisie, even if they speak every day about building 'Socialism'.

The concept of bureaucracy is not used in the same way by Max Weber. According to him, bureaucracy is not a bad thing, as it establishes an ordered system of super- and sub-ordination in which there is supervision of the lower offices by the higher ones. Such a system offers the governed the possibility of appealing from the decision of a lower office to its higher authority, in a definitely regulated manner. [26]

What is the relationship between the bureaucratic class in the Congo and its workers? Like a Janus, the bureaucratic class faces two ways. As an expression of working class ideals, it fights against exploitation of the workers: at the same time, it is interested in exploiting its own workers and ensuring their submission to its domination. Often, the product of a peasant's sale is pocketed by a parasitic class. In studying a concrete case of Comilog, Rey has shown how the neocolonial class has acted. [27]

His thesis is to see how colonial domination presents itself in a country like Congo. According to him the essence of colonial domination is industrial capital which changes through the labour market and which continuously extends. Foreign investment is behind capital. Rey's analysis is interesting because it shows the relationship between the neo-colonial class and foreign investors who work against a worker's interest.

Revamping the Old in Pursuit of the New

The obsession to create a new society in which there is no exploitation had been the origin of fighting the neo-colonial state. For this reason, people could not support Fulbert Youlou's régime. His régime, under which the Congo became independent, was, of course, the most corrupt and inefficient in independent Africa, while Youlou himself, with his propensity for showmanship, was the President least worthy of respect.

While the rate of unemployment was rising, Youlou and his ministers were living in luxury. Some of the more militant African leaders, as well as a group of Congolese students (Association des Etudiants Congolais en France) studying abroad, characterised Youlou as a 'neo-colonialist' and criticised his government for keeping the country economically dependent upon France. [28]

The most critical of the Abbé's exuberant pro-France policy was Massamba-Debat. As a result Youlou offered him a post as Ambassador to Paris, which he refused. [29] As he was involved in the people's interest, Massamba-Debat became the most popular politician in the Congo. It didn't come as a surprise when, after the riots leading to the resignation of Youlou in August 15th 1963, he was elected as President.

At the same period, the doctrine of Socialism was proclaimed as the guide for public policy. But about five years later Massamba-Debat's support for the Civic Defence Corps led to competition and antagonism between the army, which claimed the role as the authentic upholder of the revolution, and the Civic Defence Corps, which was intended to supplement the regular army and police forces and in which, its members served on a voluntary basis.

In addition, on July 29th 1966, Captain Ngouabi, officer of the Congolese Armed Forces, for unknown reasons, was arrested and imprisoned by police officers (Gendarmes). That same night elements of the army forced the police to release him. On August 29th, when members of the Youth Civic Defence Corps refused to lay down their arms and submit to army authority, Ngouabi ordered the army to attack the camp. So army troops captured the youth camp on September 1st and, three days later, the C.N.R. announced the resignation of President Massamba-Debat. [30] At the same time, Ngouabi was promoted to the rank of Major and on January 1st, 1969, the C.N.R. appointed Ngouabi as Chief of State.

CHAPTER II

Tribalism as a *Main* Problem

TRIBALISM IS NOT PECULIAR TO THE CONGO. A characteristic of conflict in many African countries is that it has been marked by African tribal struggles. Therefore it would be possible to say that tribalism is at the root of much of the political, constitutional and economic malaise and upheaval in Africa. The conflict between the Hutu and Tutsi, in the former Belgian trust territories of Ruanda-Burundi, was entirely tribal in character. The same goes for the Hausa-Ibo conflict in Nigeria.

In the case of the Belgian Congo, now Zaïre, tribalism dominated political events even before independence. For example, Joseph Kasavubu had risen to eminence as the country's political leader on an unashamedly Bakongo tribal ticket, his Party being known as the Association des Bakongo pour l'unification, l'expansion et la défense de la langue KiKongo. Moise Tshombe, the Katangan leader, was no less tribal in his political base, because of his Confédération des Associations du Katanga being primarily a political vehicle for the Lunda tribe.

In the Congo, of course, tribal antagonisms have played an important role as well. To go into politics, Youlou presented himself as a symbol of Lari renaissance and opposition to the French establishment. In the same light, when Captain Marien Ngouabi, Commander of the Congo's paratroop battalion in 1966, refused a position in Pointe-Noire, he was reduced to the ranks by Massamba-Debat Then soldiers of the Mbochi and Kouyou tribe, to which Ngouabi belonged, protested at his demotion, marching on the headquarters of the ruling political Party, and sacking it. Tribalism had changed from being a struggle to being a sinister force on 18th March 1977. When Ngouabi was assassinated, the Northern men, especially from the Mbochi and Kouyou tribes, retaliated by killing Massamba-Debat followed by Cardinal Biayenda, all from the South of the Congo.[31]

In order to explain the tribal struggle in the Congo, it is necessary to go back to the period preceding Independence. The political analysis of the Congo should take account of the tribalism aspect. Needless to say, from

Youlou to Sassou Nguesso, all Presidents have maintained a balance between tribal groups.

Tribes and Political Leaders

The question of tribalism is related to the ethnic groups of the Congo. [32] The Mbochi were regarded as the first tribe in Middle Congo to become politically prominent. Their leader was Jacques Opangault, who was born in 1907 and was trained at Catholic mission schools, first at M'Boundji and then at Brazzaville, and he joined the administrative service in 1925. This was the period when the Mbochi supplied the African cadres for the French administration as for the private sector. [33]

Another political figure who appeared in the South Middle Congo was Jean Felix Tchicaya, a member of the Vili tribe. Like Jacques Opangault, he built up his political personality on the tribe, especially the Vili tribe. After fifteen years of spectacular success, Tchicaya lost everything, his influence and his parliamentary mandate, as he preferred Paris to living in the Congo. Therefore he was replaced by Stephane Tchitchelle, his former second-in-command, [34] who moved from P.P.C. to Uddia. Later, Youlou emerged on the political scene. He understood, too, how to derive maximum advantage from the Congo tribal rivalries.

As the Lari peasants, who had refused to participate in the campaign to increase peanut production (operation arachide), ordered by the administration throughout Middle Congo, believed in Matsoua, Youlou convinced them that he was his spiritual heir. Thus he would continue his work. Considered by the Bakongo as their principal spokesman, he was elected, in 1956, Mayor of Brazzaville. In the African quarters of the city his popularity was unlimited and tens of thousands were ready to offer him not their money, but their lives. [35]

The R.D.A. (Rassemblement Démocratique Africain), realizing this early in 1957, gave up Tchicaya and made the Abbé's Party its territorial section. For this reason, Tchicaya was forced into the opposition. He then allied himself with Opangault, his long-time political adversary, and turned his back on the R.D.A. President, Houphouet Boigny, whose faithful friend he had been from 1946 to 1958.

All the examples quoted above demonstrate that the question of tribalism is not new in the Congo. The contemporary Bakongo-Mbochi antagonism reflects, of course, the state of spirit of pre-independence life. It has been said that the French colonisation, for its self-interest, needed the support of ethnic Bakongo, especially its sub-group Lari, whose members took higher positions after the decolonisation.

The replacement of Youlou, a Lari, by Massamba-Debat, a Kongo, had maintained the prominence of the South, while the rise of Ngouabi, a native of Fort Rousset, now Owando, was regarded as the retaliation of the Northern men. He was accused of offering priority jobs to the Northern men. [36] In his book entitled *Une Escroquerie Idéologique, ou au coeur du long drame*, Moudileno-Massengo expresses irritation at the exploitation of tribalism by the senior officials of the north of the Congo, in order to run the country. Is the situation really as described by Moudileno?

The Effect of Tribalism on Daily Life

Everyone in the Congo seemed to be affected by tribalism. There is no doubt that to obtain state living accommodation, a place to read at school or to apply for a job in the state enterprise, it is easy if you belong to the tribe of the person who is in charge. The criteria of merit and efficiency, which was the basis of Congolese administration, does not exist any more. In the light of all these facts one can say, when a minister is appointed, all members of his office from the people who are on the ground floor to the top belong to his tribe. Just having the men of the same tribe makes the minister feel more secure. But tribalism in itself is related to the weakness of the state sector, and increases the economic difficulties.

Lacking management know-how, men recruited on the basis of tribe can't make the economy better. Another problem brought to the fore by tribalism is the loss of authority. The notion of 'discipline' (which means the probability that by virtue of custom a command will receive prompt and automatic obedience in stereotyped forms on the part of a given group of people) doesn't work properly.

It goes without saying that the majority of members of the administration belong to the minister's tribe. Even if they don't want to work or are late for work, one can't take action against them. The same goes for the bank officer who embezzled and who then asked influential members of the government belonging to his tribe to apply pressure in order to release him. Tribalism still remains because leaders and social interests of long standing roots continue to count, and often determine the policies of so-called modern governments. [37] No one can deny that Congo political culture is marked by tribalism. It is difficult to ignore this reality. In the pre-independence period tribal feelings were cultivated for political purposes. Are there any connections between tribalism and revolution? Everyone knows that tribalism is common; but there has been little systematic study of the question of how revolution is affected by tribalism.

Tribalism and Revolution

No one would claim that tribalism in the Congo is compatible with the revolution Whenever you open the newspaper, or turn on the radio or watch the television, tribalism is strongly criticised. A Congolese Labour Party's newspaper *Etumba* mentioned that: 'If nothing is done to ban the tribalism, it is obvious that tribalism will ban the Congo from the map of Africa'. The contradiction between tribalism and revolution is underlined everywhere in the Congo.

Whatever the campaign against tribalism, the national conscience of the Congolese is not yet developed. Therefore, tribalism still remains the great problem which paralyses the political life of people.[38] To overcome this major obstacle, Eliou talks about national integration of a Congolese area. A construction of an airport in Likouala area is seen as a means of national integration, better than speeches in support of unity. Even if national integration remains vital, it is also acceptable that speeches must continue to educate Congolese people in order to change their character.

On the other hand, in the interest of revolution, the Congolese decision-makers should avoid tribalist attitudes. This does not preclude the fact that Congolese authorities are trying to do their best. Ngouabi had publicly denounced the blackmail made by the members of his tribe to ask him to appoint a civil servant on the basis of tribe. In this respect Ngouabi had been fair to his collaborators. Four out of eight members of Politburo are southern – Henri Lopes, the Prime Minister is a Quadroon whose father was a Cabindais half caste, and his mother came from the north of the Congo. Pierre Nze, a main rival of Lopes, is northern, while Louis Sylvain Goma is southern.

Today Sassou Nguesso, a convinced Marxist, has criticised tribalism feelings for political purposes. According to him, if words like 'Kouilou', 'les grands Niari', 'cuvette', 'pool', 'Nord-Sud', recall geographical and administrative realities, they are without doubt counter-revolutionary and essentially reactionary concepts as far as politics and ideology are concerned.[39] The links between tribalism and revolution are, of course, too simple. Most power figures inside the Party have tribal clientèle that they influence to retain the party ticket and win the top position in the next election.

Much still Remains to be Done

In a quarter of Brazzaville named Bakongo, an old man, quite furious, says the Northern people will not run the country forever. We have to wait our turn. 'Among the many spoken words you can hear in Brazzaville, it is all Southern people who belong to the government, for instance a former Prime Minister, Louis Sylvain Goma, or a new one, Edouard Poungui, are regarded only as collaborators. And you will be surprised to hear below the 'Djoue', it is the People's Republic of the Congo, while above it is the Republic of the Congo. [40] Why is it like this? Because politicians identify themselves with their own tribe and they pursue their own immediate interest, rather than explain the *raison d'etre* of revolution. The analyses of exploitation of tribes for political purposes are developed on page 45.

Language and Ethnic Groups: Lingala and Monokutaba

Two local languages are used in the Congo: Lingala and Monokutuba, which are somewhat similar, having been developed in trade centres. Lingala is often spoken in Poto-poto, a quarter of Brazzaville, and in the region north of Brazzaville (Ouenze, M'pila and Talangai). It is based on several languages, which are spoken by groups traditionally thought to have had a common origin. (Mongo, N.Gombe and Losengo.)

Little by little words from outside sources were used to suit the requirements of Lingala speakers. So the Kongo words 'Kulala' (to sleep) and 'Zandu' (market) became Kolala and Zando in Lingala. On the contrary, Monokutuba is widely used in Moungali, Bakongo and in the Atlantic coast (Pointe-Noire). It has no specific ethnic origins, but its basic elements were strongly influenced by the Kongo people. [41]

French was the language of the colonial administrators and became the official language after independence was achieved in 1960. French has an advantage over the ethnic language as it provides access to scientific and technical material. If French is widely spoken among the Congolese intellectuals, it appears that the ethnic and trade languages receive wider use, as the level of education for women has not progressed to the point where most wives can comfortably communicate in French.

A 1959 survey of the capital city's residents indicated that 85% spoke three or more languages, including an ethnic language, both trade languages and French. More than 25% of Brazzaville residents surveyed communicated primarily in a trade language, and only a small minority spoke French as a principal language. [42]

Some Elements of Geography and Natural Resources

The People's Republic of the Congo (popularly called Congo Brazzaville to distinguish it from the former Belgian Congo, now named Zaïre) is an African nation of about 132,047 square miles (about the size of New Mexico). A former colony of France, its capital is Brazzaville, situated on the Congo River. It is bordered by Gabon, Cameroon, Central Africa, Zaire and Cabinda (formerly a part of Angola).

The country has a tropical climate with high temperatures, heavy rainfall and very high humidity. There are two seasons: the rainy season which lasts from early April until late October and the dry season from early November to late March.

The country's mineral resources exist in a wide variety. Substantial deposits of petroleum have been found offshore and their exploitation by French and Italian companies is now a major sector of the economy, [43] to the point that the Congo is the fifth producer and exporter of oil in sub-Saharan Africa (after Nigeria, Angola, Gabon and Cameroon). There are also phosphate, potassium, zinc and iron; deposits of gold and diamonds have been found near M'Fuati and Mindouli.

Notes

1. See Samir Amin and Catherine Coquery-Vidrovich 'Histoire Economique du Congo 1880–1968,' *Anthropos* (Paris, 1969, p. 57).

2. Ibid. p. 57.

3. See *Le Figaro* du 26 Decembre 1977, 'Congo: un socialisme à l'Africaine'.

4. G. N. Guyen Tien Hung: *Agriculture and Rural development in the People's Republic of the Congo*, (Ed. Westview Press/Boulder and London, 1987, p. 7).

5. Ibid. p. 7.

6. West Africa.

7. See *Le Figaro* du 26 Decembre 1977, Op. cit.

8. Africa communist 1976, 'New way in Congo people's republic'.

9. Le Monde du 19 et 20 Janvier 1977, 'Les rapports entre Paris et Brazzaville se degradent progressivement'.

10. See *Le Monde* du 2 Janvier 1982, 'Congo 1981 – le Marxisme en question "or noir", "or vert"'.

11. See the article by Jon Swain: 'Parisian chic rivals Marxist rhetoric in people's republic of Congo'. Op. cit.

12. This explanation is given by Christophe Moukouéke, the party's Propaganda Secretary, in the *African Communist* (No. 59 Fourth Quarter, 1976).

13. Denis Sassou Nguesso: 'The Congo: Key tasks of the current stage'. *World Marxist Review*, (April 1978).

14. Samir Amin and Catherine Coquery-Vidrovitch: *Histoire Economique du Congo 1880–1968*, (Ed., p. 63. Op. cit.).

15. Ibid. p. 64.

16. Hugues Bertrand: *Le Congo, formation sociale et mode de développement économique.* (Ed. Maspero, Paris, 1975, p. 86).

17. See *Le Monde* de 2 Novembre 1979, 'le Congo après seize ans de révolution'.

18. See La Déclaration du 12 Decembre 1975, A self-criticism of the leaders of the Congolese Labour Party.

19. P. F. Gonidec: 'l'état Africain – évolution – fédéralisme – centralisation et décentralisation – panafricanism librairie.' *Général de droit et de jurisprudence*, (Paris 1970, p. 36).

20. Ibid., p. 47.

21. Karl Marx: *Selected Writings*, Edited by David McElland, (Oxford University Press, 1977, pp. 332–335).

22. Archie Marfeji: 'Neo-colonialism, state capitalism or revolution?' in *African Social Studies*, Edited by Peter C. W. Gutking, (London, 1977, p. 419).

23. Marien Ngouabi: 'Scientific Socialism in Africa, Congo Problems, Views and Experiences' *World Marxist Review* (May 1975, No. 5 Vol. 18).

24. See Jean-loup Amselle and Emmanuel Gregoire 'Complicité et conflits entre bourgeoisies d'état et bourgeoisies d'affaires: Au Mali et au Niger' in *L'état contemporain* by Emmanuel Terray (l'Harmattan Paris, 1987, p. 29).

25. Refer to Lenin in *L'état et la révolution*, Ed. Seghers (Paris, 1971, p. 20).

26. Max Weber: 'On charisma and institutional building', *Selected Papers*, Edited by S. N. Eisenstadt (The University of Chicago, 1968, p. 67).

27. Pierre Philippe Rey: *Colonialisme et transition au capitalisme. Exemple de la 'Comilog' du Congo Brazzaville*, Ed. Francois Maspero (Paris, 1971, p. 518).

28. Gordon C. McDonald: *Area Handbook for People's Republic of the Congo* (U.S. Government Printing Office, Washington D.C., 1971, p. 100).

29. See *West Africa* (June 6th 1964). 'Brazzaville enigma'.

30. Gordon C. McDonald. Op cit. pp. 104–10.

31. See Cas De Villiers: *African problems and challenges* (Vallant Publishers (PTY) Ltd., 1976, p. 85).

32. There are four principal ethnic groups: the Kongo group are in the area between Brazzaville and the Atlantic coast; the Téké live in the plateau country north of Brazzaville. The Mbochi are situated in the river area west of Mossaka and the Sangha inhabit the region of Sangha and Likouala in the far north.

33. See Rene Gauze: *The Politics of Congo, Brazzaville* (Standford University Press, California, 1973, p. 2).

34. Ibid. p. 4.

35. West Africa (August 24th 1963) 'Rise and Fall of Youlou'.

36. Le Monde du 29 Avril 1975, 'Congo: Le socialisme à petits pas ... au plus près'. Let us see that, according to Ngouabi, among contradictions which affect the Congo, tribalism is one.

37. See Irving Leonard Markovitz: *Power and Class in Africa* (Prentice-Hall, Inc., United States of America, 1977, p. 99).

38. Marie Eliou: *La formation de la conscience nationale en république populaire du Congo* (Editions anthropos, Paris, 1977, p. 72).

39. See *Bulletin Quotidien de l'ACI* (17 August 1979, p. 3).

40. See *Le Monde* du 31 Decembre 1981, 'Congo 1981 – le marxisme en question – le printemps de Brazzaville'.

41. See Gordon McDonald: *Area Handbook for People's Republic of the Congo*, Op cit., pp. 60–61.

42. Ibid., p. 61.

43. See David Hilling: *Physical and Social Geography. In Africa South of the Sahara 1987*, Sixteenth Edition (Europe Publications Ltd., 1986, England).

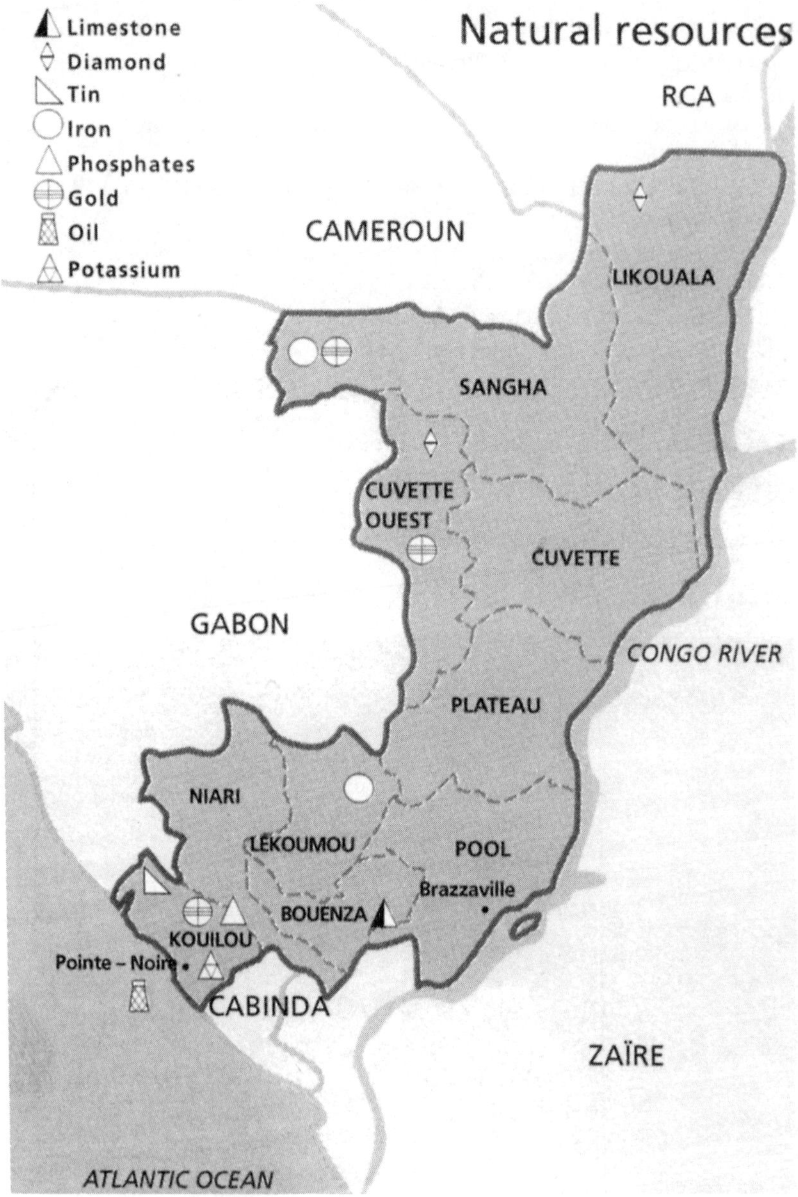
Natural resources
Limestone
Diamond
Tin
Iron
Phosphates
Gold
Oil
Potassium
RCA
CAMEROUN
LIKOUALA
SANGHA
CUVETTE
OUEST
CUVETTE
GABON
CONGO RIVER
PLATEAU
NIARI
LEKOUMOU
POOL
Brazzaville
BOUENZA
KOUILOU
Pointe – Noire
CABINDA
ZAÏRE
ATLANTIC OCEAN

PART II

Preliminary Political Change and New Way

THOSE OF US WHO ARE INTERESTED in African studies have already learnt that the Congolese socio-political evolution has traditionally been tumultuous and punctuated by periodic upheavals. Almost all changes could be interpreted as a disagreement of larger masses with the politics led by bureaucrats. The Congo has followed several steps in order to build the nation. In each step, each régime, with its leaders, justifies the path it has chosen.

It did not come as a surprise when a group of professional politicians (Jacques Opangault, Youlou Fulbert, Titchellé, etc.) regarded independence as an important step which allowed them to take control over politics. However, Youlou and his companions used state power to accumulate money, build women 'villas', and appropriate commercial opportunities.

For this reason, technocrats, trade union leaders and some revolutionaries thought the new way to build the new society was the Socialist orientation, which gives the state control of the economy. Massamba-Debat and Pascal Lissouba have been chosen for this purpose. No longer, since 1968, when opposition to Massamba-Debat and his government arose. Therefore, Ngouabi and the highly politicized army moved squarely into the middle of the political arena. [1]

From 1968 to now the country has been run by military presidents. This has nothing to do with the 'military régime'. Observers have seen the rise of Ngouabi, Yhombi and Sassou, as the dominance of the Bakongo and Laris by the northern tribes (Kouyou and Mbochi).

What happens to the Congo from the point of view of political trans-formations is extremely interesting. It has been said that the Congo is permanently politically unstable. [2] In the next part of the book attention will be focused on political changes in the Congo. What were the main causes of these changes? What do these changes bring to the country, and what are the differences between the previous régime and the new one? After more than twenty-five years of independence, why should we not look at those with the power to bring about change? Did they succeed or did they fail?

CHAPTER III

The Emergence of the First Republic (1960–3)

UNTIL SEPTEMBER 1958 it goes without saying that Congo was a part of a huge land of French Equatorial Africa (A.E.F.) ruled from the capital, Brazzaville (population 107,000) by a French Governor-General. When all four territories voted 'oui' to General de Gaulle's new constitution for 'the Fifth French Republic', and chose to belong to the French community, there were four republics on September 28th, 1958: Republic of the Congo (capital Brazzaville), Chad (capital Fort Lamy), Gabon (capital Libreville) Oubangui Chani (Bangui). The emergence of the Republic of the Congo is closely tied up with the story of one of the most unique personalities in Africa: the former Abbé and President, Fulbert Youlou.[3]

Which role did Youlou play? Pre-independence and independence politics were to a great extent the history of ethnicity and we will see how tribes were used for political purposes and how European colonization exacerbated them.

Youlou's Road to Power

Fulbert Youlou, a priest, went into politics in 1956.[4] During this period he founded the Democratic Union for Defence of African Interests (U.D.D.I.A.). No later than November of the same year, he was unanimously elected Mayor of Brazzaville. As he was shrewd and very intelligent, he organised his own Party, which rapidly drew support away from the P.P.C., called the Party Progressive Congolais. From this period politics were becoming increasingly tribal and personal, and party labels and platforms meant less to the voters than did their symbols. A Balali voted, inevitably, for Youlou's, whose symbol was a crocodile, and a Mbochi, just as automatically, for Opangault, whose emblem was a cock.

In the election to the 45 seats in the 1957 territorial assembly, the U.D.D.I.A. and the M.S.A. (Mouvement Socialiste Africain), each had 21 seats, the three remaining places going to independents. Inevitably, it led to a coalition government and to a tug of war between the U.D.D.I.A. and the M.S.A. to turn over the independents. As two of the independents had Socialist sympathies, Middle Congo's first government was headed by Opangault.[5] The clever Youlou asked for the post of Minister of Agriculture, which would provide frequent opportunities for him to tour the country and increase his public contacts and personal prestige.

A Year of Change of the Political Map: 1958

During the session of November 28th 1958, at which the Assembly proclaimed Middle Congo to be the Republique du Congo and an autonomous member state of the community, Youlou convinced a deputy of the M.S.A. named Georges Yambot to vote allegiance to the U.D.D.I.A. When the Socialist militants of Pointe-Noire learned of Yambot's defection, they invaded the assembly hall to wreak vengeance on him.

With considerable difficulty the police and gendarmes restored order, but the Socialist Assembly men refused to discuss the draft constitution submitted by the U.D.D.I.A. and then left the hall. So the U.D.D.I.A. assembly men, neatly forming the required quorum of 23, were able, without opposition, to invest Youlou as Premier and to vote the capital's transfer to Brazzaville.[6]

Decraene described what actually happened when the militants of the M.S.A. invaded the hall: 'Premier Opangault seized the microphone, with which he struck the President of the Assembly (Jayle). Then Fulbert Youlou slipped out of his cassock and in the middle of the meeting armed himself with a gun, while his friends covered the retreat of Yambot – more dead than alive – with a variety of projectiles. Having succeeded by legal means in overthrowing the Opangault government, Youlou's followers had only one idea - to get safely out of the Pointe-Noire fief of their adversaries and regain the security of Brazzaville.

'The R.D.A. councillors feverishly surrounded Fulbert at the Pointe-Noire station, some of them obviously armed. Up to the last minute they hesitated to board the micheline that had been especially chartered, for fear of their opponents' vengeance – would they be safe? But a motorized hand-car, manned by well-armed militiamen cleared the way for the autorail on the tracks.'[7]

When Youlou came to power, for political reasons he transferred many M.S.A. civil servants to different posts and sent Bakongo to occupy positions in Mbochi country. Also, in the government that Youlou set up in December 1958, no portfolios were assigned to the opposition.[8]

As the M.S.A. lost control of power, Opangault and his followers asked Mbochi and Batekes, who lived in Poto-poto, to attack the Bakongo and Laris. In February 16th 1959, tribal war broke out. This was the bloodiest that the town had ever known. The houses of the Lari in Poto-poto were set on fire. Bodies of men, women and children were strewn in the road. For days Poto-poto and Bakongo were ghost towns; only a few dogs roamed their deserted streets. Soon more than two hundred dead and four hundred wounded were reported.[9] Four French surgeons worked day and night in the new Brazzaville hospital (Hôpital Général), where they performed 60 operations in 72 hours.

In spite of the consequences of tribal war, the U.D.D.I.A reinforced its position and decided to transform the Provisional Government to the Government of the Republic. There was no doubt that Youlou became the unique leader who controlled the situation in the Congo. 1958 was a year of political change of the map. The power moved from Opangault, who controlled the Mbochi and Batekes of the North, to Youlou, who had the support of the Laris and Bakongo in the South of the Congo. The Laris and Vili were said to be more educated and received better access to education as European colonization started from the coast and spread inland. True, the Lari and Vili were more educated – it was a good enough reason to offer them the top positions. In doing so, Youlou damaged the credibility of his government. Politics is nothing else than a game of balance.

Youlou, the Father of Independence

Two years after the Republic was proclaimed, it became independent without fighting. As had been said by Youlou, independence had been achieved in peace, friendship and complete agreement with France, 'to whom we express our gratitude and affection'. He added that 'our thoughts turn towards General de Gaulle, the man of Brazzaville, the glorious creator of our freedom and independence.'[10]

Very soon after independence, Youlou announced the creation of a Government of National Union. He made clear that he would bring Opangault into his cabinet, Kikounga NGot, Germain Bicoumat and Tchicaya as well. Behind his desire for political harmony, it is obvious that a clever Youlou intended to prevent his opponents from openly criticizing his government and, at the same time, calm the tribal tensions. Did this Government of National Union work? This is another story.

During its first year in power the government took some measures in order to create jobs for youth who needed employment. It was decided to direct unskilled young towards rural occupations. To carry out this policy, a school for training civic leaders (Ecole des Cadres Civiques) was established.Unfortunately, many students expressed the wish to serve in the army rather than in the rural posts for which they had been trained.

Youlou Faces a Demand for a Second Real Independence

Much has been said about the relationship between Youlou's power and France. It is true Youlou's power represented European interests. Attention should be given to the relationship between power and the masses. Since Youlou became President, his régime had turned its back on the interests of the masses.

As has been mentioned by Bill Freund, two elements explain the African crisis: on one hand the relationship between the state and the mass of people, and on the other hand the deteriorating condition of the economy in the large majority of African countries. [11] It is clear that two elements contributed to the fall of Youlou. In Youlou's period there was no doubt that the state did not represent the interests of people. In addition, the country's economy showed no signs of progress.

Independence has been considered by the masses as the means to reach a solution to their problems. Unfortunately this was not the case. It did profit a bureaucratic class. President Youlou had made too many mistakes. Youlou's régime was, to use Chou-en-Lai's phrase, 'ripe for revolution'. The Abbé himself increased the masses' anger with his corrupt and extravagant life style, his Dior soutanes, his dubious European advisers and business friends. Another aspect which irritated people was Youlou's support for Tshombe and secessionist Katanga. [12]

Worse still, Youlou announced the establishment of a single Party. At the same time, Sekou-Touré, who had been invited to explain how interesting the single Party is, used this opportunity to arouse the Congolese Labour Unions against the Abbé's regime. Therefore, the demands for a second real independence were expressed by a joint committee of trade unions. The trade unions' demands included reform of the government, the election of a new legislature, and resignation of incompetent and corrupt ministers, notably N'Zalakanda, the Minister of Justice. As Youlou turned down all trade union demands, a general strike was called. Then Youlou retaliated by arresting two outstanding union leaders, Gilbert Pongault and Julien

Boukambou. In respect of this arrest, Youlou was treading on dangerous ground.

The Starting Point of Revolution: 1963

The main force of revolution which took place in August 1963 was the trade unions. It was said that the arrest of two leaders of the trade union and the decision to establish a single party had been the cause of the revolution, called generally, with reference to the French revolution of 1848, 'les trois glorieuses'.

Let's see the steps of this movement. On Monday, August 13th, union traders called a general strike, demanding higher wages, protesting at what they called government graft and calling for changes in President Youlou's government. On Tuesday, August 14th, a meeting took place at the railway station (la gare), surrounded by the gendarmerie. There trade unionists protested against the idea of a single party and demanded the release of the two arrested leaders.

The demonstrators went to prison. In order to turn back the demonstrators, police had to use tear gas, hand grenades, sabres and sub-machine guns. [13] Instead of stopping strikes, the demonstrators went on. Youlou called in French troops in order to restore peace, while in Paris President de Gaulle is understood to have held a Cabinet meeting to discuss the Congo situation. When Youlou saw that he had lost control of the situation, he promised to form a new government. He also decided to postpone the idea of a single party. But it was too late.

It is too late now

On Wednesday, August 15th about 7,000 strikers gathered around the Presidential Palace, shouting demands for Youlou's resignation. The French troops refused to get involved in Congolese affairs. A few hours later the top-ranking Congolese officers, Majors David Mountsaka and Felix Mouzabakany, persuaded Youlou to resign. 'Mon Général', President Youlou is reported to have said in a telephone conversation with President de Gaulle, in which the General had refused to direct intervention of French troops to keep the Abbé in power, 'I have resigned'. De Gaulle's refusal to save Youlou contrasted with French military intervention in support of Leon Mba's régime in Gabon. From that period all political changes which occurred in the Congo are the expression of the Congolese will – they cannot be attributed to French or Soviet influence.

Major Mouzabakany – A Man of the Day

If Major Mouzabakany had wanted, he could have been President, but this was not his ambition. He handled a tumultuous situation with great care. Throughout the day of August 15th Major Mouzabakany behaved as a man with a clear vision of his country's future. First of all he ensured the security of the outgoing President and then he called for the constitution of the provisional government.

He also called on the Congolese army to restore order and to save the ministers' houses, instead of leaving them to be set on fire by the angry masses. By giving his resignation to Major Mouzabakany, a clever Youlou wanted the army to take over instead of the trade union. At the end of the day Mouzabakany ordered some Congolese troops to pick up Massamba-Debat from his native village, Mboko. The new government was going to be led by him, former Minister of Development and President of the National Assembly, who found himself in disagreement with Youlou. Was Massamba-Debat the right man? Why did the army refuse to take over? It was said the army was not prepared politically to run the country. On the other hand the army did not play a significant role in the overthrow of Youlou. The main force, if not the only force, which had called for Youlou's resignation was the trade union.

Massamba-Debat with the New Men

Unknown men were called very quickly by Massamba-Debat to serve as ministers in his Cabinet. It seemed like a paradox because none of the trade union members belonged to the Cabinet. Only technicians were required to handle the situation left vacant by the overthrow of Youlou.

All men lacked political experience, and some of them were either moderates or revolutionaries. As soon as it was formed, the new government manifested its desire to remain a member of the Union Africain et Malgache (U.A.M.), the Organisation of African Unity (O.A.U.), and it affirmed its friendship with France.

It also announced the release of all persons jailed for political reasons by Youlou's régime. It was said that an enquiry should be made about the financial administration of Youlou's regime. According to official sources, Youlou invested 30 million francs C.F.A. (about £40,000) in Europe. Other ministers are also believed to have transferred funds. [14]

Some ministers were arrested: Sathoud and Gandzion, respectively

Ministers of Industry and Education, while Marcel Ibalico, President of the National Assembly, escaped to Leopoldville. Youlou himself was being held prisoner some miles out of Brazzaville. As Youlou had gone, a new team was going to create the conditions of prosperity of the Congo. Socialist orientation was seen as a good thing for the population. Did the new men bring prosperity? The reality behind the apparent Socialist orientation was that few objectives were attained.

Table 1: Composition of the provisional government	
Head of Government and Defence Minister	Alphonse Massamba-Debat
Minister of the Interior and Information	Bicoumat Germain
Minister of Justice and Civil Service	N'Kounkou
Minister of Finance, Mines and Transport	Edouard Babackas
Minister of National Economy Planning, Public Work and Post Office	Paul Kaya
Minister of Health, Labour, Education, Youth and Sports	N'Galiba
Minister of Foreign Affairs	David Ganao
Minister of Agriculture	Pascal Lissouba

In fact a simple change of team does not of itself solve all the problems of the country. Apart from good intentions, the government was not able to orchestrate a radical change in the economy and the political structure. Worse still, the technocratic view had been overrated at the expense of political will.

CHAPTER IV

The Revolutionary Period

FOR THE CONGO, Socialism was the only alternative to the dramatic situation left by Youlou's regime. Therefore the new régime, led by Massamba-Debat, had adopted the doctrine of 'Scientific Socialism' as the guide for public policy. Institutions reflecting Socialist principles were established. The Congo was going to become one of the revolutionary states of Africa. The choice of 'Scientific Socialism', as pointed out by Lissouba, was completely different from 'Utopian Socialism', which, under the pretext of defending humanity, considers both the wealthy and the poor man as human beings. [15]

Pascal Lissouba, who represented the hard line, and other Marxists, exercised much influence on Massamba-Debat and forced him to opt for a policy advocating 'Scientific Socialism', not for any 'African Socialism', which refers to the 'negritude'. In this sense, when Massamba-Debat paid his first official visit to Ghana, he said at the Vinnela Ideological Institute, that the Congo was fighting against capitalists and colonialists who want to become perpetually rich at the expense of African poverty. '... if this struggle is to be effective, then we must have African unity'. [16] The Socialist option was based on the government's belief that the state will provide the welfare. It was a political expression of an emerging consensus that Socialism was more perfect than capitalism in practice. The question raised was who should make decisions on the way society allocated its resources – the state or the individual.

The M.N.R. as the Centre of Political Power

To lead the country toward Socialism, many young revolutionaries, under Massamba-Debat, decided to establish a single party. This was paradoxical. After all, it was the idea of creating a single party which had caused the clash between Youlou and the trade union!

As soon as Massamba-Debat came to power, he began to do what he had criticised Youlou for doing. The M.N.R. became a single party and the centre of all power. Why did Massamba-Debat contradict himself? Was the single party the only solution that could drive the country to Socialism? Apparently history has taught us that the need to build a nation and to promote the creation of a new economy led the African states, independently of their doctrinal positions, one after the other to choose the single party.

This is not to say the single party has the same functions and pursues the same objectives in the African states. It is inevitable that in some cases the single party was involved in the defence of the interest of people; in other cases the single party has to represent the interest of a minority. The important point is that in Youlou's view the single party would work at the expense of the people. It thus concentrated the power in the hands of those who represented the interest of imperialism in the periphery, while in Massamba-Debat's vision, the single party was an instrument of integration of all the people, as the common enemy was colonialism and imperialism.

It follows from what has been said earlier that the goal of the single party differs from one to another. It cannot be limited to form new élites, to create a new ruling class, to unite and to shape the political leaders capable of organizing the country, on the grounds that the masses cannot themselves govern. [17]

This élitist view of the aim of the single party as expressed by Duverger is radically different from the view expressed by Fanon, who disagreed with the conception according to which the masses cannot govern themselves. [18] Fanon's analysis is relevant to understand the difference that exists among the single-party groupings in the African States. So far, all single parties consider themselves to be parties of the people. This indicates that the nature of interest of any given single party is the same as that of the people. The reality lies in what has been said about the relationship between single party and the people.

We have a low opinion about the justification of the single parties in Africa. Their principal aim was to defend their own interest rather than those of the people. They supported the people not in the interests of social justice, but because they wanted to concentrate power in their hands and to use the whole wealth for their own interest. The rise of the single party has been accompanied by an increase of inequality of wealth at the expense of the people. This might be because the government's intentions are different from the revolutionary ethic, which requires in some degree self-sacrifice, altruism and the subordination of individual desires and welfare to the greater good.

The MNR as a Marxist Party

Massamba-Debat [19] was elected General Secretary of the M.N.R. and President of the Republic, while Pascal Lissouba, a brilliant scholar, was appointed Prime Minister. Leon Angor, well known for his admiration of the Chinese revolution, was appointed President of the National Assembly. One had the impression that the hard line, or the proponents of Marxist ideology, grew stronger.

As the M.N.R. had adopted the Socialist path, there were no surprises when the delegates of the congress of 1964 denounced the free enterprise system as inefficient, and called for the control of state on foreign trade. In the manner of other Marxist parties, all organisations of the masses: the Youth of the National Revolutionary Movement (Jeunesse de Mouvement National de la Revolution); the Revolutionary Union of Congolese Women (Union Revolutionnaire des Femmes Congolaises); the Congolese Trade Union Confederation (Confédération Syndicale Congolaise) depended on the authority of M.N.R.

Throughout all the period of 1964 the M.NR. reinforced its power. Moderate ministers like Paul Kaya were sacked. At the same time, the nationalisation of education and youth movements became an urgent task. Ties with Communist countries, especially the Soviet Union, China and Cuba, were developed at the expense of France. There was no doubt that Socialism was seen as incompatible with liberal societies. One of the central prongs of the attack on the capitalist system was the belief that it will continue to exploit the periphery.

The J.M.N.R.: Revolutionary Enthusiasm and Delinquency

The J.M.N.R. was the official youth movement and the youth left-wing of the M.N.R. In its origin the J.M.N.R. intended to supplement the Congolese military forces against events threatening the Congolese revolution. Supported by Massamba-Debat and trained by the Cuban experts, the J.M.N.R. became a potent force which ensured the security of the masses.

Little by little, the goal of ensuring security which had characterized it at the beginning of the revolution had evaporated, being replaced by acts of vandalism such as searching cars of diplomats accredited to the Congo or trying to arrest people on a merely arbitrary basis. Some of the young men who used to belong to the Civic Guard (la Défense Civile) were involved in political liquidations. The victims were Joseph Pouabou, President of the Supreme Court and Lazard Matsocota. A climate of fear surrounded the population. One reaction to the perpetual J.M.N.R. harassment was the withdrawal of the U.S. Embassy from the Congo. [20]

Radical Politics go on

There is no doubt that the purge of moderate ministers had reinforced the power of the militants of the J.M.N.R The replacement of Bicoumat by André Hombessa as Minister of the Interior, the appointment of Claude

N'Dalla as Secretary of State of Youth, marked the triumph of the J.M.N.R. In the light of the radicalism, the Congo had rejected the Ocam's denunciation of Ghana's subversive activities in April 1965.

The first five-year plan (1964-68) was announced, followed by the introduction of central planning and the nationalization of the means of production. At the same time, the Congolese authorities had decided to nationalize private schools. Relations with the other Congo, now Zaïre, were getting worse and worse, as Tchombe endorsed Youlou's exile in Leopoldville, before he moved to Spain, where he died.

The M.N.R., as the single party, took control over the government. Therefore Pascal Lissouba[21] who was always so keen on Marxist doctrine and the freedom of the government, had to adopt a conciliatory attitude towards his friends of the M.N.R. and the members of his own government. Lissouba, who saw that the actions of his government were very limited, had resigned his portfolio as Prime Minister.

Apparently his resignation confirmed the supremacy of the pro-Chinese members of the M.N.R. In April 1966, Noumazalaye, a new protégé of Massamba-Debat, became Prime Minister and General Secretary of the M.N.R., with the sole responsibility of bringing more radical progress towards Socialism. A new government had been created, whose many portfolios were offered to the advocates of radical policies.

The High Price of Massamba-Debat's Errors

The error of Massamba-Debat was that he did not maintain the balance of power between the armed forces and J.M.N.R. Ideologically and militarily trained by the Cubans, the Civic Guard claimed the role of saving the revolutionary Socialists in Congo from their enemies. Therefore, it considered the army, police and gendarmerie as forces related to the colonial era. True, the gendarmerie had released Youlou and helped him to escape to Leopoldville, where be was in exile before going to Madrid.

The ascendancy of the Civic Guard affected the army, who saw its role as the authentic upholder of the revolution decline. Therefore, conflict arose between the two forces. Massamba-Debat didn't do anything to defuse the situation. On the contrary, he supported the militants of the Civic Guard and offered them more privileges (Such as facilities to obtain free lodgings and donations from sympathetic Eastern embassies in Brazzaville)[22] than the military. By doing just the same, be got into trouble with the armed forces, who never approved the ascendancy of the J.M.N.R.

Massamba-Debat's first error was to underestimate the army. Some officers, among whom was Ngouabi, took advantage of this situation to arouse opposition among the military against Massamba-Debat. Instead of negotiating with the officers and reassuring them that the army remained the authentic force which ensured the population's security, Massamba-Debat ordered his Prime Minister to arrest Ngouabi and demoted him from the rank of captain to that of a simple soldier.

For this reason tensions increased between the government and the armed forces. While Massamba-Debat was attending a O.C.A.M.'s meeting in Tanarive, Ngouabi supporters in the army barricaded the headquarters of the J.M.N.R. in demonstration against Massamba-Debat's decision to arrest him.

To avoid violence from soldiers, the Prime Minister, Noumazalaye[23] moved with the members of his Cabinet to the 'stadium revolution', insisting on the protection of the Cuban faithful to the government This unrest forced Massamba-Debat to release Ngouabi. While Massamba-Debat was facing the military opposition, he got rid of some militants of the M.N.R. This may have been Massamba-Debat's second error.

It is obvious that while Massamba-Debat was President, his task was not made any easier by the revolutionaries in the central committee of M.N.R., whose members might agree with his overall purpose but not necessarily with his methods or the speed with which he led the revolution. By sacking his younger lieutenants (Noumazalaye, Lissouba and Leon Angor), Massamba-Debat forced them to make what alliances they could with the leftist wing of the army, with the result that the army won much sympathy from them.

The Consolidation of Power

The year 1968 had been characterized by the consolidation of power by Massamba-Debat. He reshuffled the government and reduced the power of the M.N.R. leaders. For instance, Noumazalaye was removed from his post as Prime Minister, as well as André Hombessa from his post as Minister of the Interior and head of the powerful youth.

In the days that followed, Massamba-Debat combined the power of the President and those of the Prime Minister. Worse still, he appointed people to high-ranking posts not on the basis of Marxist-Leninism but according to friendly relationships. For instance, a non-Marxist, like Lieutenant Poignet, was made Minister of National Defence. Then Massamba-Debat became moderate in a country which had opted for the Socialist road. He should have avoided anything like that because he antagonised the extreme Marxists as well as the army.

Like his predecessor, Youlou, he was unable to achieve the unity of all forces. When his régime became oppressive, Massamba-Debat lost his popularity and his personal integrity. Tensions between him and several Marxists increased. In addition, anonymous leaflets attacking the President were distributed. To put an end to this situation, Massamba-Debat offered to resign if an alternative candidate could be found; but no one came forward. This was followed by demonstrations in support of Massamba-Debat, who had announced the dissolution of the National Assembly; the suspension of activities of the political bureau of the M.N.R. While he seemed to control the political situation, Massamba-Debat left Brazzaville for his home village (Boko).

The Power Struggle has Begun

Under the careful patronage of Massamba-Debat, the moderate factions had increased their power. In his speeches, broadcast on the radio, Massamba-Debat strongly criticized the young people who represented the hard line of Marxism in the Congo.

The young Marxists, led by Noumazalaye, former General Secretary of the M.N.R., had been defeated, at least temporarily. However, a strong counterbalance of Marxists, whose influence through the country seemed stronger than the moderates, had warned the militants against Massamba-Debat's deviation.

It was generally accepted that the political ideology issues had been the main reason for the power struggle between the extreme left, represented by the Civic Guard (la défense civile), and the moderates. A shrewd Noumazalaye started to meet the leaders of the armed forces and to conclude an alliance. It was agreed that to save the country from non-Marxist orientation, it was necessary to open an ideological conflict with Massamba-Debat.

There is no doubt that behind the ideological quarrel there were, besides, many personal struggles. Instead of making an arrangement with all Marxist leaders, Massamba-Debat revived the issue by asserting his authority. To cut a long story short, be didn't want to know about what had been said by those who thought that the country must be run on Socialist ideals only. For instance, Pascal Lissouba, who was the first leader in the Congo to believe in Marxism, insisted that 'Scientific Marxism' would not be abandoned. There was no indication that the army would participate in the political game. Because of the lack of unity among Marxist leaders, the senior officers of the army became a burden on Massamba-Debat's shoulders.

At the time of Noumazalaye's appointment as premier minister, Ngouabi, as the army's representative on the M.N.R. central committee, openly attacked Massamba-Debat in the central committee. For such behaviour Massamba-Debat disliked him. Apparently, Ngouabi's criticism of Massamba-Debat was centred on the J.M.N.R., who were trying to force the army into a submissive position and reduce its political force. As an example of a good officer, Ngouabi was the first to speak out against Massamba-Debat's blockage of the revolution.

A Burden on the Shoulders

Less enthusiastic than they had been during the events which took place in 1963, the military leaders started to complain about Massamba-Debat's deviation. As Massamba-Debat's politics had aggravated the security problems and encouraged the arbitrary arrests in the country, the Saint-Cyr Coetquiddam officer groups became more and more worried. They (the military leaders) also warned him against the moderates who didn't share the idea of change. Massamba-Debat felt he was not receiving any support in his drive for the revolution at a time when the army appeared as a burden on his shoulders. It was clear he was facing the chance of defeat because of opposition from both the left of the party and the army.

Unhappy Marxist leaders, like Noumazalaye, Lissouba and Leon Angor, joined the armed forces to overthrow him. Massamba-Debat, who feared being deposed by the coalition of the left and the army, left Brazzaville for his home village. At the same time, the extreme leftist, Captain Ngouabi appointed himself Commander-in-Chief of the army, and appeared to be about to take over the government.

Once again, like Youlou, Massamba-Debat gave his dismissal to the military. The upshot was that Lieutenant Poignet was appointed the Head of State. The following day, Ngouabi, who was the big boss of the country, appealed to Massamba-Debat to return to office, assuring him of the protection of the army.

So he had to return to Brazzaville, ending Lieutenant Poignet's short-lived presidency. At the same time, Ngouabi set up the constitution of the new government such that the military would play a major role. Captain Alfred Raoul, generally regarded as a 'front man' for Captain Ngouabi, had been appointed Prime Minister, Major Felix Mouzabakani was offered the position of Interior Minister. While the Government Departments had taken some measures to improve the economic situation, Ngouabi went further by announcing the creation of the C.N.R. (National Council of the Revolution). As Jean Pierre N'Gombe pointed out, the C.N.R. was seen as the formation of a political organization committed to Scientific Socialism. [24] While the M.N.R. seemed like a mass movement with all tendencies, the C.N.R had leanings towards Scientific Socialism.

The C.N.R. as a Significant Turning Point

In order to rekindle the flame of the revolution, the C.N.R. became to some extent an *avant-garde* party, whose main missions were to guarantee the continuity of the revolution. Captain Ngouabi, who was President of the C.N.R. and Commander in Chief of the Army, was undoubtedly going to become Head of State.

In the same period, politics were dominated now by the coalition of the leftist Marxists, and the officers of the army. Among the leftist Marxists were the two former Prime Ministers of Massamba-Debat (Lissouba and Noumazalaye). Ngouabi deliberately conferred on C.N.R. the power to appoint the Prime Minister and other members of the government, at the suggestion of the President. To avoid criticism of his opponents on all sides, Ngouabi said, 'The C.N.R. is not working against somebody; so those who hate its acts commit anti-revolutionary acts'.

Why is the C.N.R. a significant turning point? Because it represents three bases:

For the first time, since the independence of the country a military man became leader of the state, [25] with the consent of both the armed forces and the large number of progressive intellectuals. According to Obenga, the political figures around Ngouabi included Pierre Nze, Noumazalaye, Lissouba, Martin Mberi, Justin Lekoundzou Ithi Ossetoumba, as well as military officers like Nicolas Okongo, Sassou Nguesso, Yhombi Opango and Gaston Eyabo. [26] Both Noumazalaye and Lissouba have supported Ngouabi because of divergences that existed between them and Massamba-Debat.

For the first time in the nine-year history of the Congo, the power moved from the South to the North. The South had lost its pre-eminent position to run the country.

For the first time the idea of an *avant-garde* party which could pave the way to Socialism emerged.

These three elements are related to the political change. At one level, one can explain things in terms of the consolidation of the military régime. In the struggle for power between Massamba-Debat and Ngouabi, it is clear that Ngouabi won the presidency, both in terms of personal confidence in the military and policy divergences.

At another level, the linkage between tribes and personal influence can be seen as having determined the political change. The installation of Yhombi on the throne is seen as a way of keeping the power in the hands of the North. There was nothing to do about the confidence of the armed forces and the Marxists. At the final level, however, class conflict could play an important role. This can be illustrated by what happened in 1979, when Sassou Nguesso, the leader of the militant faction of the Congolese Labour Party, became the Head of State.

As we have already indicated, Congolese political change comprises a number of very different elements. There are substantial overlaps between ethnic, personal antagonisms and class conflicts. All society was affected by these various components. The impact of the relationships between society, culture and personality as they affect, and are affected by, political change has been underlined by James R. Scarritt in his conceptual framework of political change called a 'Control and Facilitation'. [27]

But this study doesn't use 'control and facilitation' to explain the political change. So far, there's no control of politics by tribalism, ideology or by the military régime and the facilitation of these factors by politics. The Congo's Marxism or Socialism is an exceptional one as all factors already enumerated play an important role. To master all these factors is very difficult. The political history of the Congo reveals that sometimes tribalism plays an important role; sometimes ideology also plays a dominant role, and sometimes personal antagonisms influence the course of politics.

What Does the Concept of Change Mean?

Change could be interpreted as the passage of one form to another. It is nothing to do with the quality or the quantity. We talk about change when what did exist yesterday doesn't exist today.

A nice example is the weather. We usually say the weather changes when we notice that the weather is not the same any more. What is true for the weather is also true for politics. The concept of change is vague, because it is often related to the quantity and the quality. In this perspective, the question arises: what is the nature of the change?

Speaking about the concept of change, Gonidec, a remarkable figure of the African political scene, makes a distinction between quality and quantity. For him, the accession of African countries to independence is a qualitative change as it puts an end to the legal domination of the colonial power. Unlike the quantitative change, it does not affect the deep-seated nature of

39

the phenomenon. For instance, reforms implemented in colonized countries prior to independence were able to attenuate colonial domination. [28]

Seen in this sense, the concept of change is used in referring to the concept of progress. This does not work in the case of African countries where *coups d'état*, rather than real revolution, are dominant, and there is little change which brings new structures of policy. So the concept of change should be seen in the specificity of African countries. In the context of the Congo it is difficult to judge whether the revolution of 1963 had brought a substantial change or not. It is clear from this period that the Congolese leaders have adopted a hostile attitude to imperialism; the whole political structure has changed. Yet when the revolutionaries gained power, their acts did not match their statements. One of their principal arguments was that the government's action had been blocked by imperialism.

Ideological Culture and Tribal Culture

It is important to note that in all African political systems there are at least two cultures, the ideological and the tribal. The first could be described as a belief system that explains and justifies a preferred political order for society, either existing or proposed, and offers a strategy for its attainment. [29]

This culture is expressed strongly in the Congo. Almost all youngsters and several political leaders share the ideological culture. Since 1963 they understood that 'Marxist Ideology' was necessary to guide their actions and to organise movements. The ideological culture is as much interested in explaining how men do behave in politics as it is in recommending how they ought to behave.

Nelson noted that societal life requires that members be joined and Ideology helps them to join. As such, Ideology performs an important instrumental function for the society. It performs similar functions for political movements, seeking to change the social order. For Nelson, [30] Ideology can be grouped under the heading of five functions: first, as a political belief system, Ideology provides a cognitive structure – a formula of ideas through which the universe is perceived, understood and interpreted.

The second function of ideology is to provide a prescriptive formula; a guide to individual and collective action and judgement. It is a set of rules regulating how one may act in politics, specifying the goals which may be pursued and the means used to pursue them.

Third, Ideology functions as a tool of conflict management and integration at the personal level, Ideology functions to help the individual cope with the conflicts within himself and with others, giving wholeness to his life by integrating the various aspects (roles) of individual life.

Fourth, self-identification is defined through Ideology. So, Ideology is not only a lens through which men see their world, but it is also a looking glass in which they see themselves and a window through which others see them. Ideology is the way men and nations define and see themselves, and hope that others see them and interpret their actions in its light.

The final function of Ideology is to serve as a dynamic force in individual and collective life, providing a sense of mission and purpose, and a resulting commitment to action.

The tribal culture is formed by the attitudes which encourage and exacerbate tribal links. In that case, as we continue to see in some respects, some appointments in the Congo to the top positions might be decided on the tribal basis. These attitudes provoke the motives of doubt and frustrations among young intellectual and efficient workers, who see political leaders as representing only the interest of the particular ethnic or communal group to which they belong.

Today, the leaders are facing two problems: ideological culture and tribal culture. Even if the Ideology is the official guideline of the political system, there is no doubt that the tribal past continues to weigh heavily on the attitudes of leaders. The two cultures can affect the political change.

Table 2: Congo: Ethnic representation in cabinets, 1960–67 (in percentages)				
Ethnic Group	As % of population	Independence Cabinet	Prior to 1963 coup	Massamba-Debat 1967 cabinet
Bakongo	47	43	57	50
Bateke	20	7	7	10
Mbochi	11	21	21	10
Mbeti	7	—	—	10
Sangha	5	7	7	—
Others	10	23	7	20
Source: Donald Morrison *Black Africa*. (p. 213)				

As men rationalize their class interests, these interests motivate efforts to retain or change the order of society. Beside class interest, there exist certain other values that men pursue: some men prefer income, and others power or privileges; others may pursue still different values such as virtue, justice or ambition. That is why people with the same class interests often differ politically. People with different class interests often hold similar political beliefs, and act similarly in politics. The two cultures are linked and have influenced the course of events in the political scene.

Table 3: Members of the Cabinet of the Congo	
Colonel Louis Sylvain Goma	Prime Minister
Mr Pierre Nze *(N)	Minister of Foreign Affairs
Major Francois Xavier Katali *(N)	Minister of the Interior
Captain Florent Tsiba *(N)	Minister of Information
Mr Henri Lopes *(N)	Minister of Finance
Mr Victor Tamba-Tamba	Minister of Labour and Justice and Keeper of Seals
Mr Moundele N'Golo (N)	Minister of Land Improvement, Construction and Housing
Mr J. Baptiste Taty Loutard	Minister of Culture, Arts, Sports and Scientific Research
Mr Antoine N'Dinga-Oba (N)	Minister of National Education
Mr Gabriel Oba-Apounou (N)	Minister of Youth
Mr Hilaire Mounthault	Minister of Transport and Civil Aviation
Mr Rodolph Adada (N)	Minister of Mines and Energy
Mr Marius Mouambenga (N)	Minister of Industry and Tourism.
Mr Jean Itadi	Minister of Rural Economy
Mr Pierre Moussa (N)	Minister of Planning
Mr Joseph Elenga N'Gaporo (N)	Minister of Trade
Mr Pierre Damien Boussoukou-Boumba	Minister of Health and Social Affairs

* Denotes member of the Political Bureau of the Congolese Labour Party. The Political Bureau is the country's highest political authority.

N Denotes the Northern members of the cabinet.

Note: President Colonel Denis Sassou Nguesso* also holds the portfolio of Minister of Defence.

Note: Needless to say, from Youlou to Nguesso history has taught us that the tribe to which the President belongs is the one whose cabinet members are dominant.

Under the cabinet, following Yhombi Opango's eclipse in February 1979, eleven out of seventeen of the members of cabinet were northern. See Table on previous page.

The Model of Political Change

This model of political change contains two factors which could explain enormous changes which occurred in the Congo. Two factors have been distinguished. Factors which facilitate political change are related to ideological culture and tribal culture. Factors which govern political change are related to class interests and personal values.

Ideological culture + tribal culture
In return political change influences
ideological culture and tribal culture

Factors which facilitate political change

The class interest + personal values

Factors which govern political change

The study of the political change of the Congo tells us that class interest and personal values are the main causes of change: the conflicts which occur inside party or government are related to the rationalization of the interests that some men pursue. To put these conflicts down only to Ideology or Tribalism would be over-simplifying the analysis of the political change in the Congo.

Self-interested Individuals

The goal of public policy, according to the revolutionaries, is to achieve the greatest good for the greatest number. The principal matter on the agenda in the early stage of the revolution was social justice and greater equality in the distribution of wealth. The previous régime (Youlou's régime) was seen as a major contributing factor to poverty and inequality and therefore incompatible with social justice. Observations tell us that the concept of social justice and the emergence of the welfare state lead to a concentration of power in the hands of a few individuals. The outcome has been that collective actions have been sacrificed. This brings us to the crucial point: there is no dispute with the idea that politicians are self-interested individuals; they often maximise returns just like the businessman. Obviously the contents differ from those in the market place. That politicians maximize different objectives is not subject to discussion. Behind the revolution many

Congolese revolutionaries pursue their own goals: fixed standard of living or an assured place in society. Like the market, the Party is therefore incompatible with an unwavering commitment to the type of egalitarianism and social justice which forms the basis of Socialist societies. The market is driven by the prospect of gain, and this implies inequalities in the distribution of wealth. The Party is doing the same.

The Congolese Labour Party's members behave like the sellers in the market. They use speeches to persuade masses about the necessity of the revolution, which helps them to satisfy their needs. Needless to say, in the market the sellers tend to persuade the consumers about the quality of the product. The consumers are sovereign, whereas in politics the play of vested interests and patronage rule. The markets, like the Party, lead to gains for some at the expense of others. It cannot be denied that the poor are subsidising the leisure of the Congolese Labour Party's members. As one can see, the difficulty in guaranteeing social justice is related to the self-interested individual.

If the revolution failed to meet its objectives, it is simply because Congolese politicians are self-interested individuals. It is not the fault of the 'Socialist option': the Congolese Labour Party has a faith in the Socialist option, without knowing what kind of sacrifices are required.

Notes

1. See Samuel Decalo: *Coup and army rule in Africa* (Newhaven and London, Yale University Press, 1976, p. 123).

2. A good analysis of the political instability in the Congo is given by Paul Antillon in his excellent *Thèse d'état* at the University of Grenoble.

3. See Rolf Italiaander: 'Fulbert Youlou of the Republic of the Congo. A priest becomes President.' In *The New Leaders of Africa* (Prentice-Hall, Inc. Great Britain, 1961, p. 169).

4. Fulbert Youlou was born on June 8th, 1917 in Moumbouolo (Brazzaville district) the son of a trader of the Balali tribe. After studying at elementary schools in the French Congo, he entered a Catholic seminary in Akono, French Cameroon. He completed his studies for the priesthood in Brazzaville, was ordained in 1946, and became a parish priest in Brazzaville. Fulbert Youlou is officially unmarried, but he appears to have many wives and numerous children. The Catholics regard him as traitor, while others say he is immoral.

5. Virginia Thompson and Richard Adloff: *The emerging states of French Equatorial Africa* (Sandford University Press, Standford, California, 1960, p. 486).

6. Ibid. p. 489.

7. See *Le Monde* du 23 Janvier, 1959.

8. Two Europeans, Kerherve and Vial, were named respectively ministers of Industrial Production and of finance, and Tchitchelle was given the key post of Minister of the Interior.

9. See Rolf Italiaander: 'Fulbert Youlou of the Republic of the Congo, A Priest becomes President'. Op. cit. p. 172.

10. Events reported by Rene Gauze in *The Politics of Congo Brazzaville* (Standford University Press, 1973, p. 175).

11. Bill Freund: 'The making of contemporary Africa' *The development of African society since 1800* (Indiana University Press, Blomington, 1984, p. 251).

12. Reported to *West Africa*, 13th August 1973, 'Brazzaville. Ten years of revolution'.

13. See *West Africa*, August 17th 1963, 'Riots in Brazzaville'.

14. West Africa, Saturday 24th August 1963, 'New men in Brazzaville'.

15. See *Le mois en Afrique*, Novembre 1966, numéro 12, 'Socialism congolais. Le point de vue de Pascal Lissouba'.

16. See *West Africa*, June 6th 1964, 'Brazzaville Enigma'.

17. Duverger, M: *Political parties* (London 1965, p. 257).

18. According to Franz Fanon, in an underdeveloped country the Party ought to be organized in such fashion that it is not simply content with having contacts with the masses. The Party is not an administration responsible for transmitting government orders; it is the energetic spokesman and the inalienble defender of the masses. In order to arrive at this conception of the Party, we must above all rid ourselves of the very western, very bourgeois and therefore contemptuous attitude that the masses are incapable of governing themselves. See Franz Fanon *Les dammées de la terre* (Paris 1961, pp. 139–145).

19. Massamba-Debat Alphonse, born in 1921 in the Boko region. He was Bakongo. He went to primary school in Boko, and then was trained as a primary school teacher in Brazzaville. With the outbreak of war, he went to Fort Lamy in Chad, and taught there. He became headmaster of a primary school in Mossendjo (his Prime Minister, Pascal Lissouba was born in the same town in 1931). Later, in 1959, he was elected to the National Assembly and, holding his first significant political office, became its President. Youlou later brought him into the government as Minister of State in 1961, and then Planning Minister.

20. Samuel Decalo: *Coups and Army Rule in Africa* (Yale University Press, Newhaven and London, 1970, p. 14).

21. Pascal Lissouba was Massamba-Debat's Prime Minister from 1964 to 1968. He had devoted himself to politics with unselfishness, human kindness and optimism. For him in the context of the Congo, tribes are related to classes. So his thesis: tribes, classes.

22. Samuel Decalo: *Coups and Army Rule in Africa* (Op. cit. p. 150).

23. Noumazalaye Ambroise, succeeded Lissouba as Prime Minister in April 1966 and Massamba-Debat dismissed him in January 1968. Born September 23rd, 1933 at Brazzaville, he received his M.A. in Mathematics at the University of Toulouse. While in France, he married a French woman and joined the Communist party and the

FEANF. He interrupted his advanced studies at the Institut National de Statistiques for political reasons.

24. Jean Pierre N'Gombé: 'Towards a new upsurge of the revolutionary process' *World Marxist Review* (Volume 20, No. 9 September 1977).

25. See *Le Monde* du 2 Janvier 1969, 'Congo-Brazzaville Commandant Ngouabi deviant chef de l'Etat'.

26. Theophile Obenga: 'la vie de Marien Ngoubi 1938–1977' *Présence Africaine* (Paris 1977, pp. 46–47).

27. James R. Scarritt: *Analysing political change in Africa. Application of new multi-dimensional framework* (Westview Press, United States of America, 1980, p. 4).

28. Pierre Francois Gonidec: *African politics* (Martinus Nijhoff, The Hague, 1981, p. 6).

29. See *Ideologies and modern politics*. Edited by Nelson (first published in Great Britain, 1972, p. 7).

30. Ibid. pp. 16 and 17.

The Eruption of the Military into the Political Scene

ALL OVER POST-INDEPENDENCE AFRICA a similar scenario unfolded. African countries started with civilian régimes and they ended up with military ones. The only exceptions were rare cases like the Ivory Coast and Senegal. In only a decade, in Algeria, Burundi, Central African Republic, Congo Brazzaville, Congo Leopoldville (now Zaïre), Dahomey (now Berlin), Ghana, Mali, Nigeria, Sierra Leone, Togo, Uganda; several *coups d'état*, some bloodless, others violent, transferred the power into the hands of revolutionary councils or welfare committees composed of members of the army or police forces.

Military intervention is seen as the manner of bringing order into the administration, eliminating corruption, making swifter and better provision for the needs of the community, and for the requirements of the department of the country. [1]

Those who are interested in studying the eruption of the military in the political scene have mentioned that the causes of intervention vary from one case to another. An empirical case study of the Uganda coup, led by Michael Lofchie, indicated that the army acted in order to protect their economic privileges against the Socialism experimentation. [2]

So, we can admit here that personal values and class interest have determined the political change. Lofchie's interpretation or explanation is based on the fact that as the military officers enjoyed a high level of income, they would not have accepted in any circumstances a régime which threatened their interests. Robert Price argues that the separation of the civilian and military spheres of responsibility could explain the 1966 Ghanaian coup. [3]

Taking Price's argument word for word, it means that if the role of the army had not been reduced to coming to the defence of the military professionalism, it would not have turned against the civilian régime. Samuel Decalo goes further, arguing that, despite appearances, the charge of corruption is used to justify the military intervention. It is rather personal ambitions which are the main reasons for eleven African coups which occurred between 1963 and 1972. [4]

Decalo deals with the personal aspects which provoke friction among authorities, but he neglects other aspects. The lack of spirit of particularity leads him to draw a common explanation of the eleven African coups he has studied. The absence of homogeneous African test cases. explains the difficulty of evolving a commonly acceptable explanation. Another contribution to understanding military intervention has been made by Samuel Huntington. According to him, what explains the military intervention is the nature of the political, economic and social structure of society. [5]

Claud E. Welch has attributed to the military some professionalist characteristics, which require the army to get involved in politics and to save the country from corruption. [6] In exploring the causes which have contributed to, or encouraged. The intervention of the African military in post-independence politics, J. Gus Liebenow has mentioned the weakness of political parties as a primary factor. [7]

That personal ambitions have played a great role is beyond doubt, but my own opinion, which differs from Decalo's explanation, is that military intervention in the Congo can be considered as the struggle for power on the basis of class interest. In 1968, Ngouabi acted as a leader of the leftist-Marxists, who regarded Massamba-Debat as a moderate. The military coup of July 1968 was the military's Marxist and the civilian's Marxist response to the blockage of the revolution. As Ngouabi said himself, the entire population joined the revolutionary rising of July 31st, 1968 to save the revolution. [8] Decalo has overrated personal struggle to the point of forgetting that there were a lot of differences between Ngouabi and Massamba-Debat about the revolution.

Ngouabi, or the End of the Civilian Supremacy

In July 1968, a military coup d'état put an end to the civilian supremacy, in order to put down a basis for a constructive development. A paratrooper, Ngouabi, whose personal charisma swept the armed forces off their feet, concentrated all the power into his hands. [9]

What was especially significant was the fact that a great number of military officers went into politics. Strictly speaking, there was no such thing in 1963 but gradually the army reached the high point of politicization. In such a way it challenged the civilian régime. The amount of political involvement among army officers is not the same in all countries. In some it is considerable, in others middling, in yet others nil, in some even negative. In any case where this excess is considerable, the take-over of power by the army reaches the Marxist régime. In this respect, the Congo and Benin are the best examples.

Taking up the case of the Congo, we must bear in mind that when Massamba-Debat ceased to administer the State in accordance with the principles of Marxist-Leninism, the military emerged as ruler. There is one way in which the change occurred in the Congo at least since 1963: the lack of accordance with Marxist ideology as it has been practiced in the Congo. What we say is true for Massamba-Debat, but the same is also true for Yhombi Opango. To try to legitimize their claims to rule and to stifle opposition, some leaders openly talk about a Leninist approach.

Marxist-Leninism and Scientific Socialism are in some respects regarded as the only choices available for the revolutionary élites in Mozambique, Angola, Ethiopia, Benin and the Congo People's Republic. Despite the claim of Scientific Socialism, economic performance does not seem linked to an ideological model. The increase of inequality remains considerable and the ideal pursued by the rulers to improve the welfare of rural masses and workers remains to be demonstrated.

Each change enhances the rhetoric of Scientific Socialism, yet it should deal with the difficulties encountered by the great number of poor. One has the impression 'plus ça change plus c'est la même chose'.

An *Avant-garde* Party and the Progressive Elements of the Army

It has been generally believed that the first leaders of the 1963 revolution were the trade unions but they were weak; some under Catholic influence, others oriented towards France. The absence of homogeneity weakened understanding of the revolution's objective. The common denominator seemed to be a creation of the National Revolution Movement (Mouvement National de la Révolution) at a congress in 1964.

Very generally speaking, this heterogeneity challenged the eventual chance of the success of the revolution. Even Noumazalaye, as its leader, multiplied the intrigues to isolate the progressive elements. This caused maximum awareness of the need for a new, more radical organisation. Hence the creation of the National Council of the Revolution (Le Conseil National de la Révolution) by Major Marien Ngouabi, its leader. It brought together three viable elements, civilian revolutionaries, the 'Civic Guard'[10] and progressive elements within the army. The next step was the creation of the Congolese Labour Party. This background seems to us very important to understand the impact of the military on politics. As the leader's Party was a military one, inevitably this intensified the political role of the military, at the expense of civilian authority.

In spite of the military ascendence, Ngouabi wanted to open the doors of the Party to the non-military members, to co-opt a wide range of civilian politicians and technicians whose skills were necessary to deal with the day-to-day concerns of society. What is interesting to note is that the eruption of the military on the political arena did not damage the influence of the Party. The interests of army and the Party were not opposed. Many times the Party required the military's leader to relate their way of acting to the Party's orientations.

Table 4. Military Members of Political Bureau	
President of the Central Committee of the Congolese Labour Party	Major Ngouabi*
First Secretary	Claude E. N'Dalla
Second Secretary in Charge of the Presidency of the Council of State	Major Raoul*
Other Members	Ange Diawara*
	Pierre Nze
	Justine Lekoundzou
	Ange Poungui
	Kimbouala-NKaya*

Source: Africa Contemporary Record B 419 1969–70
*Military Members of the Political Bureau

The Legitimacy of Military Intervention

It is obvious that military intervention is intended to enhance the power of the army in society. Hence, it is very difficult to recognize that military leaders are disposed to help their fellow citizens. The military leaders assert that their intervention has popular support. What would lead them to conclude that? As J. Gus Liebenow said, what kind of test can be used to validate this assertion? (He adds that dancing and demonstrations at the announcement of a successful coup are not reliable indices!) [11]

According to Liebenow, neither the women who danced in Accra in January 1966, as N'Krumah's opponents were being released by the new military government, nor the labour strikes that greeted the Ethiopian coup, are the signs of legitimacy. This remains subject to question. Large masses of Ghana and those of Ethiopia were satisfied with the military's actions.

We are convinced that in the Congo, Ngouabi had based his legitimacy on the restoration of Marxism. He had received popular support. It follows, from what has gone before, that the military coup in some respects received popular support. This is not to say all military coups are always supported by the people. This was not the case in the military coup in Burkina Faso which followed the assassination of Captain Sankara. Military intervention is not a bad thing in itself. Since the army has been politicized, the representatives of the military have shown more enthusiasm in defending the interests of the masses. It is clear that in Africa there are two types of military intervention; one is revolutionary and another is counter-revolutionary.

The Military and Plots

The difficulties encountered by Ngouabi were caused by the military. The surprising thing was the discovery in February 1969 of the plot led by Major Mouzabakani (who at the time was Minister of the Interior) and his aide, Lieutenant Pierre Kikanga. [12] The plot was not followed by the support of the armed forces. The questions raised by this plot remain unanswered. Apparently, one can discern two reasons. On the one hand, Ngouabi who was determined to restore the Marxist revolution, had expressed his hostility to the 'reactionaries' in the armed forces. This attitude had exacerbated the tensions in the army. The plot was a reactionary military response to Ngouabi's desire to speed up the revolution. On the other hand, the plot was seen as a retaliation by the Laris. In this respect, Major Mouzabakani [13] and Lieutenant Kikanga had acted on the basis of tribal interests. These are only assumptions and should not be taken as the gospel truth. No one in the Congolese Labour Party endorsed Mouzabakani's actions. It makes one realize that the army is politicized and there is no way to support someone who disagrees with the Party's line.

After the arrest of several alleged plotters, including Major Mouzabakani, Ngouabi indicated that a large network of 'reaction' had been destroyed and, he added, 'it is a network of the valet of the Abbé Fulbert Youlou'. [14] Far from easing the tumultuous situation, Ngouabi faced another one led by Lieutenant Kikanga [15] and thirty armed men across the river from Kinshassa, on March 23rd 1970. Kikanga succeeded in penetrating to the radio station of Brazzaville, multiplying the statements that he had already overthrown Ngouabi's government. A few hours later the situation was reversed.

The army, which remained loyal to Ngouabi, took control over the situation and, after few hours of fighting, Kikanga and his men were killed. One of the great reasons advanced as underlying this plot was that Kikanga acted on the behalf of the imperialists who wanted to rid the Congo of a Socialist régime. As far as we know, Kikanga was not happy with Marxist ideology. Kikanga's weak point was to have forgotten that Ngouabi had the full control of the army, which saw Kikanga's action as a threat to its interest. What would have happened if Kikanga had succeeded? Certainly the senior Marxist's officers would have been sacked. Another thing would have happened. The Congo would have moved from the Socialist experience to the restoration of the Capitalist system. The lack of military support and Socialist conviction had been the main cause of Kikanga's failure. Once again the army had shown its dissatisfaction with those who wanted to destroy the Party's interest.

The February military coup, led by Lieutenant Ange Diawara, cannot be put on the same level with the two previous coups. Diawara is well-known as one of the more extreme members of the Congolese left faction. Decalo's analysis of Diawara's challenge is related to ideological dispute and to personal power.

This analysis seems to us relevant to understand what happened on February 22nd. When Ngouabi came to power, he had a poor knowledge of Marxist literature. [16] A group, constituted by Noumazalaye, Claude-Ernest N'Dalla as well as Bongou Camille and Combo-Matsiona, could thus make a better claim to be the possessors of revolutionary truth. Yet conflict there certainly is, be it at the difference of approach about policy, or the clash between Ngouabi's style and Diawara's followers' style.

As nothing moved quickly, Diawara convinced the leftist members of the Party to overthrow Ngouabi. Once again, the army remained loyal to Ngouabi. It will also be remembered that Lieutenant N'Gollo had to play a crucial role to avoid the plotters, to take control over the Mpila's camp. When Ngouabi returned to Brazzaville from Pointe-Noire, he was informed of the entire situation by Yhombi Opango, who was responsible for forestalling the coup. The question arises: why did the army not follow Diawara? Simply because the movement of M22 was limited and did not earn the support of the whole army. Also, the situation was not ripe to overthrow Ngouabi. The army top officials like Yhombi, Sassou Nguesso and N'Gollo remained close to Ngouabi.

What was sure to happen finally did. Several plotters were arrested, and some of them were killed. The revolutionary court under the chairmanship of former Foreign Minister, Henri Lopes, delivered its verdict in the trial of the February plotters. Four were sentenced to death. Thirty-six others were given sentences varying from one year's prison to 30 year's forced labour. Eight others were acquitted, including a former Prime Minister, Pascal Lissouba. Sylvain Bemba, the writer, who had been Minister of Information for only one month before his arrest in February. He was given a three-year suspended sentence. Five students, who admitted contact with Diawara, were directed to voluntary work 'in agriculture'.

The court had 20 judges including the Supreme Court President, Charles Assemekang and Pierre Nze, Member of the Political Bureau of the Congolese Labour party. President Mobutu was accused of helping Diawara. According to President Mobutu, the charge that he had been helping Diawara was 'simply provocation', and that he 'could not be the friend of anyone who, when he visited Brazzaville, would not even shake my hand'. [17]

Diawara and his comrades, whatever differences arose inside the Party, should not have challenged Ngouabi outside the Party. By using arms, they contravened the Party's principles. Ngouabi exploited this error in such a way that he eliminated a potential source of opposition. Why did Diawara and his colleagues choose to fight outside the Party? What the M22 should have done was to earn the majority inside the Party and to overthrow Ngouabi. It was said, during the day-to-day meeting of the Political Bureau, that Diawara and Nouamazalaye had often instructed Ngouabi on the finer points of Marxism. Thanks to Nzé, Ngouabi was able to counter-attack. It is clear that Ngouabi needed Nzé for tactical and opportunist reasons, but he could not save him from the purge of 1975.

Political and Military Implications

After having expelled the members of the plot from the Party and from the Central Committee, Ngouabi enhanced his power in the Party, in the State as well as in the army, by appointing his staunch supporters like Nzé as a Vice-President and a literary prize winner, Henri Lopes, as a Prime Minister'. [18] Yhombi Opango, a moderate and liberal, was promoted from Major to full Colonel, the highest rank in the army since independence. Also, he was co-opted as a member of the Politburo. To put an end completely to the opposition, Ngouabi went further by making a decree which integrated the police into the army. So all police business was to be handled by the People's National Army. [19]

The infantry battalion which had been responsible for the attempted coup, was placed under the same command as any other branch of the National People's Army. At the same time, Ngouabi decided to reorganise the Central Committee's permanent commission to the army. Formerly it was under Lieutenant Diawara; a decree gave it to Ngouabi.

The year following the *coup d'etat*, Ngouabi regarded Yhombi Opango as powerful, and very dangerous to his own power. Hence, he removed Colonel Yhombi from his function 'as General Chief of Staff' of the Congolese Army and appointed him as Inspector General of the armed forces. Captain Victor N'sika Kabala took over. What is important to bear in mind is the fact that the structure of the high command of the army made Ngouabi Commander in Chief of the Armed Forces, followed by the President of the permanent commission of the army, Captain Denis Sassou Nguesso, and the first political commission of the army, Lieutenant Goma Foutou. [20] Needless to say, the removal of Yhombi weakened Ngouabi's own support among the northerners.

Civil Opposition to Ngouabi's Power

As it is my intention to analyse all the opposition encountered by Ngouabi, we must observe that he was threatened, not only by certain officers of the Congolese armed forces, but also by left-wing colleagues who got involved in Diawara's *coup d'etat*.

Nine years of power showed that Ngouabi was not able to restore stability. In less than two years following the coup d'état of February 22nd 1972, the trade unions and, futhermore the students, posed constant threats of disruption. These threats were only dissipated by arrests and constant harassment of militants by the armed forces.

The two main political figures were Anatole Kondo, Chairman of the Congolese Trade Union Federation and Jean Jules Okabando, First Secretary, Congolese Socialist Youth League. The opposition was provoked by the fact that the trade unions and the students were not satisfied with Ngouabi's practices. Students demonstrating in 1971 and again in January 1974 led Ngouabi to dismantle the U.G.E.E.C. It is important to note that the youth regarded Diawara with admiration because he was an excellent officer and he was anchored to Marxist theory. This being so, some left-wing members of the Party and the youth continued to express their sympathy with him. To set things right, Nouabi called, in July 1972, a Party Congress. [21]

According to him, the Central Committee was at the mercy of a particular group and was not an effective revolutionary vanguard. In the same spirit, he had written a programme for one party, which was approved in December 1973. [22]

Getting to the Root of Things

The year 1975 opened with the observation that much needed to be done in order to impose a correct political line, and to rescue the revolution from the 'complacency and lethargy' of a bureaucracy which, despite repeated purges, continued to show a tendency towards bourgeois values rather than Socialist activism. [23]

With this in mind, an Extraordinary Meeting of the Central Committee was held. As a result, there was the declaration of 12th December 1975, announcing a decision to 'radicalize the revolution'. On paper, the Congolese Labour Party claimed to run the country on the basis of 'Marxist-Leninism' and used the slogan 'all power to the people and only to the people' ('tout pour le peuple rien que pour le peuple'). In practice, things were different. No one took the responsibility to say the Party was not doing its job properly. It was a political taboo. This was the first time the Party had decided to criticize itself and to confront its lack of efficiency. In deciding to reveal the problems of the Party, Ngouabi wanted to guarantee to the people the continuity of revolution. He had already done similar things in 1972, throughout the emergency Congress of the Congolese Labour Party. At the time he commented upon the wide gap between theory and revolutionary practice. [24]

'All power', the Congolese Labour Party promises, 'belongs to the people'. After many years, the people are demanding what is supposed to be theirs. For Ngouabi, the time had come to eliminate all the evils undermining the country and blocking the process of revolution. The surprising thing was that when the Party was doing poorly, it was Nzé or Lopes' fault. When the Party was doing well, Ngouabi claimed the success. We should not dismiss Nzé and Lopes without also dismissing Ngouabi. No one understood why the major victim of the purges was Lopes as he was the *head* of the purge commission set up in September 1975! Why did Ngouabi appoint him if he had known Lopes had 'bourgeois behaviour'.

What is Wrong with the Party?

In 1975 Ngouabi behaved paradoxically by criticising strongly his party followers. He himself used to claim that 'at the stage of National, Democratic and People's Revolution, we are not Socialist yet'. He added, 'Our Party is still young. So we must understand and forgive the efforts of its members'.

The second paradox is that by denouncing his followers who were not speeding up the revolution, Ngouabi confirmed in some respects the criticisms made by Diawara and his followers, although they were considered as 'gauchistes'.

It should be observed that the declaration of 12th December diagnosed the difficulties encountered by the Party and the State. It denounced the weakness of party leadership, lack of liaison between the leadership and the masses, the irresponsibility of the trade unions, the inflexibility of the state apparatus, the weakness of the state economic sector, the excessive number of workers in state enterprises and the incompetence and irresponsibility of cadres. [25]

After recognising its inefficiency, the Political Bureau resigned, the important figures like Nzé, the Party's chief ideologist and Lopes [26] were removed from their positions. Only Jacob Okandza still remained the Director of President's Office. In order to prepare for the Congress of the Party which would provide it with the new revolutionary structures capable of leading the revolution, the Revolutionary General Staff (l'Etat Major Special Revolutionaire) was established: a new revolutionary cabinet was formed.

By sacking the members of the Political Bureau for their inefficiency, Ngouabi earned their dislike. The same is true for some officers of the armed forces. Ngouabi faced two problems: first he needed different kinds of revolutionaries in the Party, who would work hard to implement the objectives of the revolution; second, many of his predecessor's revolutionaries did everything to prevent the Congress being held. It does not come as a surprise when, Ngouabi, while addressing a meeting with his special revolutionary general staff (Etat Major Special Revolutionaire), [27] heard some workers shouting: 'Why shouldn't we change the locomotive as well as a carriage?' President Ngouabi counter-attacked by saying, 'the radicalization is a dynamic elimination, without ambiguity, or sentimentalism about all the sickness diagnosed at all levels of the state'. Ngouabi promised to continue the revolution and to restructure the Party, saying: 'The Central Committee continues to exist. The function of the Secretariat and Politburo are temporarily being exercised by the Special Revolutionary General Staff (l'Etat Major Special Revolutionaire), until the next extraordinary Congress of the Party, which will give the Congolese Revolution a new, efficient and truly revolutionary political leadership: new Central Committee, Politburo, Central Committee Secretariat members.' The radicalization raised some problems which remain unsolved.

For instance, one such problem was how to make the administration efficient with a full control of the Party over it. On what criteria would the new leaders be appointed? Should they be in the Party as well as the State? So far the administrative rationality and the ideology were not going hand in hand. One should bear in mind that a movement of radicalization had reduced the number of the members of the Party. The workers' strike following the declaration of 12th December again allowed Ngouabi to sack some leaders of the Party.[28]

Whereas between 1975 and 1976 a special Revolutionary General Staff was working very hard to reach the Congress which would bring the new structures, some members of the Party, threatened by radical measures, tried to stop the course of progress.

What Ngouabi did not realize was the fact that he considered the movement of radicalization as a solution, not as a problem. Since more leaders were inclined to bourgeois values, he should not have believed radicalization would work without difficulties. For many, Ngouabi himself could not be regarded as a good example. To discredit him, it was said: 'who purged whom' (qui épure qui)?

Like his predecessors, Youlou and Massamba-Debat, Ngouabi was unable to restore the unity of his turbulent Party. He contradicted himself and many purges undertaken by him made the Party too weak. In addition, the Revolutionary Cabinet (le gouvernement révolutionaire) did not possess the financial means to implement its policy. There was no way that the country would be able to create enough jobs for its population. Therefore the gloomy economic situation increased the people's anger. Ngouabi multiplied un-convincing speeches like this: 'We did not fail, but we did not succeed' (nous n'avions pas échoué, maits nous n'avions pas réussi). Only God knows whether people believed him or not.

It is true, Ngouabi had difficulty in restoring the vitality of the economy. He fell into ideology's trap of neglecting the economy. One thing could happen, if he was not assassinated, he could have been overthrown by his followers who had supported him.

The Second Military Period or Yhombi Era

On March 18th 1977, Ngouabi, who had taken power in a coup nine years earlier, was assassinated in his palace. This was the first time such a thing had happened. This being so, another chapter was written in the Congo's turbulent political history.[29]

Day after day, many versions emerged of Ngouabi's assassination. According to official sources, Captain Kikadidi was said to have killed Ngouabi to allow Massamba-Debat to take over. Another version was given by Jos Blaise Alima. He considered that what had happened was the outcome of an intense power struggle between the two ethnic races, Mbochi and Bacongo.[30]

According to him, Massamba-Debat and Ngouabi agreed on the mechanics of the handover: a Commando Squad was to kidnap Ngouabi from the presidential palace and escort him to a hiding place outside Brazzaville, from where he would announce his resignation in favour of the former President. If it was agreed that Massamba-Debat sent Kikadidi to escort Ngouabi, why should Kikadidi kill Ngouabi? Why had Massamba-Debat, if guilty, waited quietly at home to be arrested?[31]

A week later, after Ngouabi's death, what was sure to happen finally did, Massamba-Debat was executed. In addition, four soldiers, including a member of Ngouabi's bodyguard, Corporal Ontsou, who was said to have fired the fatal shot, were among those executed. Two days later, the Archbishop of Brazzaville, Biayenda was executed by Ngouabi's family members. It was said that the Archbishop had visited Ngouabi shortly before the attack and used 'magic powers to neutralize his "invulnerability"'.[32]

The Death of Ngouabi: The end of one step and the beginning of another

Having been removed from the Central Committee and the Political Bureau for being too bourgeois, Yhombi never inspired confidence among the workers, youth or the farmers. Back in March 1977, it was inadmissible for the left-wing members of the Party to regard him as their President. Tchystere Tchicaya, who was in charge of party headquarters, one of Ngouabi's heirs, was prone to attack the right-wing dictator's Yhombi. Why did they select Yhombi? To answer this question we need to see the background of Ngouabi's assassination. Yhombi was Kouyou like Ngouabi. To prevent tribal tensions, it was necessary to choose Yhombi as a President because the official version of Ngouabi's assassination said it was Kikadidi, a Lari, who killed him. In that context, it was clear that tribalism had played a crucial role. If the constitution had worked properly, the President of the National Assembly should have been President at least temporarily.

Among those who were regarded as Ngouabi's successors were Sassou Nguesso and Sylvain N'Goma, both pro-Soviet. Why? The answer is very simple: because both were members of the special revolutionary general staff and, among other things, they were the top militiary leaders able to control the army. It is worth noting that in the hours following the assassination of Ngouabi, it was Sassou Nguesso who signed the official communiqué of the military committee of the Party. According to Sassou Nguesso, Marien Ngouabi found his death in combat with weapons in his hand on Friday 18 March 1977[33]. The selection of moderate and liberal Yhombi, in less than two weeks, was a surprise.

The political situation was getting worse and worse. The truth is neither Sassou Nguesso nor Sylvain N'Goma could run for the presidency, at least in such circumstances. To avoid tribal tensions, they made an apparent compromise with Yhombi who belonged to Kouyou's tribe, like Ngouabi. This compromise weakened Yhombi, as it was Sassou Nguesso who had the real power. Political observers came to the conclusion that the political influence and ideological commitment of Yhombi's group were inferior to those of the Sassou Nguesso group, and that it was just a matter of time before the latter would gain power.

The State Under Military Rule

As Ngouabi was assassinated, the highest officers in the armed forces made claims about maintaining order and wanted to conduct the burial. For this purpose, temporarily, Tchystere Tchicaya, a Party Headquarter member, (permanent du parti) gave full power to the military and named the military committee.[34]

Yhombi became its President, while Sassou Nguesso and Sylvain N'Goma both received high cabinet positions. As soon as Yhombi took over power, he declared on 6th April to keep the Socialist path for which President Ngouabi gave his life. A week later, he contradicted himself. On 12 April he announced the Fundamental Act, which abrogated Ngouabi's 1973 constitution.

Subsequently all the people's regional powers which Ngouabi defended did not exist any more. Three days later, he gave an interview in which he said that any influence exerted by 'the first Socialist country (the Soviet

Union) would only be beneficial to these struggling countries of Africa'. It did not cross his mind that all decisions were opposed to the party line. [35]

The other side of the coin was that on an arbitrary basis, he decided to cut the salaries of some workers. He took another step with the announcement of increasing international aid. He went to Gabon, France and Libya and sent personal delegations to China, West Germany, Italy and Belgium. He reassured the Americans of his intention to improve diplomatic ties, and agreed to discuss compensation for Mobil and Texaco, whose holdings had been expropriated.

The Military Committee's Dictatorship

This was the first time in the Congo's political history that the country was run only by the military. Far from improving its relationship with the members of the Party, the military committee was haunted by maintaining all the powers in its own hand, and Yhombi Opango, as head of it, acted as a dictator. None of his predecessors had done what he finally did. He restored rigour as the way in which he could reduce the difficulties encountered by the country, but he did not himself set an example.

He kept the workers waiting for three or four months to receive their take-home pay. Did he do that on purpose? One thing was sure: he did not like the Socialist orientation. By giving the salaries to the workers only once every three months, Yhombi expected to persuade them that Socialism was not good at all.

Using force, instead of taking into account what the common man thought, Yhombi wanted to frighten the people. By banning the National Assembly and the people's powers, (les pouvoirs populaires), Yhombi showed that he did not like the Party's interference in the political scene. In preferring an ordinary Party Congress to an extraordinary one, he wanted to move to another party, perhaps completely different from the Congolese Labour Party. Party members' anger mounted as Yhombi took the direction that contrasted with the Party's orientations.

The Congolese Labour Party as the Main Loser

The Congolese Labour Party (P.C.T.) has paid the price of its own errors. Many personal conflicts of its leaders, and some purges, have weakened it. So far, the differences of analysis in the Party were devoted to strengthening the revolution.

Since Yhombi took over, there was a clear contradiction between the right-wing line incarnated by him and the left-wing one incarnated by Sassou Nguesso. While the Party was the centre of power before Ngouabi's assassination, it became less powerful under Yhombi. Also, the top ideologists of the Party were sent to the villages. [36]

In addition, the Party officials got the blame for bureaucratic formalism, inertia, inefficiency and self-satisfaction. [37] Such criticism did not seem relevant to the Party officials, who did not recognise Yhombi as a revolutionary. As Yhombi ran the country according to his own will, the powerful personalities of the Party urged the overthrow of Yhombi's rule. Therefore, in 1979, a small group of the military committee under the control of Sassou Nguesso, expressed the desire to summon the meeting of the Central Committee. Needless to say, the military committee members close to the Party (Tsiba, N'Gollo, Katali, N'Goma) supported Sassou Nguesso, while Yhombi had only two loyalists, Ebacka and Anga, also from Owando. Tchystere Tchicaya and Goma Foutou, both Yhombi's rivals, accelerated the process that would give great power to the Central Committee. [38]

They criticized publicly on television how Yhombi's practice contrasted with the goal of the Party. Yhombi himself made people hate him. At the beginning of his power, he retained his legitimacy by ascribing himself and the Party to the cause of Ngouabi. Very soon he gave up what he had finally promised. He made some errors, such as his decision that employees who were non-permanent teachers at the Marien Ngouabi University were to cease receiving payment for the classes they gave.

In a country which had opted for Marxism, the behaviour of Yhombi was not acceptable. There were no slanders and lies orchestrated about him. According to Ekondi Akala, the Party put out lies about Yhombi in order to get rid of him. We can safely say that things were more complicated than he thought. [39] Influential members of the Congolese party had exploited Yhombi's own ostentatious way of life to overthrow him.

Clientalism as a Means to Maintain the Power

The first point that should be made is that, whereas the principle of holding the Central Committee meeting was accepted, Yhombi was preoccupied with the problem of how to be elected by the P.C.T. politicians. Tchystere Tchicaya and Florent Tsiba, the main architects of the popular demand for the convening of the Central Committee session on 5 February 1979, had already convinced the majority of Central Committee members. If Yhombi was a good Communist and politician he should have refused the Central Committee meeting's demand, and created the balance of power in his favour inside the Central Committee. Another option was to destroy the influence of Tsiba and Tchicaya by accusing them of blocking the military committee's efforts to restore the economy. He did not and allowed the Central Committee to take place.

As Machiavelli said, a ruler who wants to maintain his power is often forced to act immorally. [40] Yhombi finally did what Machiavelli taught. It should be remarked that at this point, he wanted to gain power by using clientalism. By clientalism, is meant here the personalized relationship between patrons and clients commanding unequal wealth, status, or influence based on conditional loyalties and involving mutual benefits. Clientalism is also related to the ethnic identity.

The P.C.T. politicians close to Yhombi were corrupt. It is said that Yhombi gave them envelopes containing money in order to be elected at the meeting of the Central Committee. This rumour was confirmed at the meeting which Bokamba-Yangouma held on 31 January 1979 at the railway station. [41] Rightly or wrongly, some top leaders of the Party were dismissed in this affair. They were widely labelled 'les envelopés'. As the outcome of the meeting (sessions) of the Central Committee, the conservatives or the right wing, led by Yhombi, had been defeated and Yhombi himself was asked politely to relinquish power. The Central Committee approved Sassou Nguesso's succession. [42] Could anyone even dream that the Central Committee would tell Yhombi one day that he didn't suit them and should resign? By doing so, the Central Committee has shown how it was the centre of power. Should Sassou Nguesso learn lessons from what happened to Yhombi? Does Sassou Nguesso run a similar risk? What happened yesterday, could it happen today? Compared to Yhombi, Sassou Nguesso had the control of the Central Committee, the youth and the armed forces.

The Third Military Period or Sassou Nguesso and the Return of Orthodoxy

The military committee was divided between Yhombi Opango and Sassou Nguesso. It was clear that N'Gollo, Florent Tsiba, Xavier Katali and Sylvain N'Goma provided a majority for Sassou Nguesso. As the first Vice-President in charge of party matters as well as Defence Minister, Sassou Nguesso was clearly in control of the military and the centre of party plots against the relatively a-political President. [43] It didn't come as a surprise to see Sassou Nguesso take over. [44] Since the assassination of Ngouabi, he was considered as his real successor. And the fundamental law (l'acte fondemental) has shown how powerful he was. [45]

It should be noted that Nguesso's arrival as President of the Congolese Labour Party was regarded as a return to orthodoxy. It was a clear indication of the ascendancy, not only of civilians over the military, but also of the militants over the moderates. [46] This is well shown by the appointment of Tchystere Tchicaya as the Congolese Labour Party's official ideologist, Camille Bongou, the main representative of the movement of 22nd February, as Secretary General of the Central Committee to the Presidency, and the trade union boss, Bokamba Yangouma.

It seemed obvious that the time had come to require the leftist-Marxists to speed up the process of the revolution. [47] By opening the Party to all the factions, Sassou Nguesso undoubtedly wanted to achieve the unity of the Party. But the broader question which faced Nguesso was: to what extent was the unity of the party possible?

Towards the Unity of the Party

Sassou'Nguesso may be said to offer unity in the Party, where neither Massamba-Debat with the M.N.R. nor Ngouabi with the P.C.T. succeeded. The unity of the left forces remains the corner-stone of the Party's stability. To some extent unity is undermined by ideological and ethnic aspects. In Ngouabi's period, the militants were divided and were deeply self-interested. This being so, they sacrificed the interest of the Party. The purge of the Central Committee and the Political Bureau as well had aggravated the divisions. To make the Party more efficient, Sassou Nguesso called for unity.

In this respect, all left-wingers joined him. When the Congress of the Congolese Labour Party was held at the end of March, he was appointed Head of State, President and Chairman of the Central Committee.

He enjoyed a personal triumph, because he expressed the will to continue the revolutionary rhetoric in Ngouabi's style. In this respect, he invited the Congolese to go to the polls in 1979, for the first time since 1973, to adopt a new constitution and elect members of National Assembly and People's Council. There was no doubt that it was a return to the revolutionary structures shelved by Yhombi.

It is absolutely true that Sassou Nguesso led the Party to unity. It is nevertheless important to note that the Congolese Labour Party was facing purges from time to time. This makes us think that behind the apparent unity there were personal and political conflicts in the higher reaches of political power.

Unity for How Long?

One thing is certain. Since Sassou Nguesso came to power, his position had not been completely secure. He felt threatened by his colleagues, both in the Party and in the army

In 1979, if Sassou Nguesso was the winner, there was no doubt that Tchystere-Tchicaya, Nzé, Lekoundzou, Tsiba, Xavier Katali, Sylvain N'Goma, and Yamgouma became the most important and influential political figures in the country. All of these personalities claimed their role in 1979. All of them were potential competitors for presidency.

For instance, Florent Tsiba became one of the most serious challengers. He is reported to have reproached Sassou Nguesso for not being more radical. And Xavier Katali, reportedly Moscow's key man, shared Tsiba's point of view. [48] This being so, the elimination of Tsiba weakened Katali. [49]

Tchystere-Tchicaya, number two of the Party, whose influence was increasing in the party, represented much risk to Sassou Nguesso. Wishing to avoid this influence, Sassou Nguesso appointed Daniel Abibi as a Central Committee Secretary of the Congolese Labour Party's Political Bureau. Needless to say, when Nguesso travels abroad, he prefers to leave Bongou Camille in charge instead of Tchystere-Tchicaya.

As for Abibi, [50] his political star rose when an ideological document he prepared (especially critical of Tchystere-Tchicaya), caught the President's attention. It is said that Abibi provides the President with a radical alternative to an exclusive tactical alliance with M22 against the hard line.

The next step was the elimination of Tchystere from the Central Committee, and subsequently he was arrested on grounds of complicity in the 1982 bombings. [51] The Vili lost their dominance in the Party, as Tchystere was regarded as the second most important political figure, [52] even if Louis Sylvain N'Goma was still Prime Minister. [53] What happened to Tchystere-Tchicaya was not new. In the history of the Congo it is almost acceptable to remove the second political figure. Massamba-Debat did the same with Pascal Lissouba and Noumazalaye, while Ngouabi did the same with N'Dalla Graille. Perhaps if Yhombi Opango did the same with Sassou Nguesso, he would have stayed in power. The political system in itself does not accept that the second political figure becomes influential. That is why Sassou Nguesso is trying to undermine Camille Bongou's position to the point that he will ban the position of Party Headquarter Secretary (Sécrétaire permanent du parti) at the next P.C.T. Congress in July 1989. Camille Bongou has just lost control over the Party to a Sassou Nguesso faithful, André Obami-Itou.

Political Games and Alliances

As a good Marxist-Leninist, Sassou Nguesso has maintained balance among regions in the extreme Northern Imphondo-Sangha. Because of the fact that Pierre Nzé and Xavier Katali became dangerous, Sassou Nguesso appointed Daniel Abibi from the same region as Nzé, in order to keep the support of the Sangha.

By rehabilitating Ambroise Noumazalaye as a Minister of Industry and Manufacturing, Sassou Nguesso maintained his popularity in the Imphondo area It is clear that Noumazalaye represents an alternative to Katali. He has the advantage of being independent of the Soviets. He is also much less of a risk to Nguesso, since, unlike Katali, he is not a military man.

The appointment of Edouard Poungui, the new Prime Minister, and other Niari potentates like Pierre-Damien Boussoukou-Boumba (Minister of Scientific Research), Dieudonné Kimbembé (Minister of Justice) and Celestin Goma-Foutou (P.C.T. Secretariat member in charge of Ideology) contributes to reinforcing Sassou's position in the Niari region.

In the past, there were complaints from the Niari that the region was not represented in the power structures, since Lissouba was regarded as a main rival of Ngouabi but Nguesso offers a new answer. Since the exclusion of Florent Tsiba from the Political Bureau, the Batekes resent the domination of the Cuvette region. To reduce the gap of this domination, three Bateke were given ministerial posts: Ambroise Gombouele (Trade and Consumption); Dr. Christophe Bouramoue (Health and Social Affairs); Dr. Ossibi Douniam (Fisheries).

The other major alliances for maintaining power are the presidential manoeuvres in the Vili region. The fact that Sassou Nguesso's wife is Vili seems to increase his popularity in this area. However, he maintained Vili politicians in important posts: Hilaire Mountault, Minister of Transport and Aviation, Jean-Baptiste Tati Loutard, Minister of Culture and Art, and Bernadette Bayonne Mountou, Minister for Basic Education.

The region of Cuvette is another instrument of political games and alliances. The Mbochi people are more prominently represented in the government, especially members from Sassou Nguesso's home village, Oyo. Is there something wrong? In the political history of the Congo, it is always like that.

What Sassou is doing had to be done by his predecessors. Cuvette ministers are Justin Lekoundzou, Ithi Ossetoumba (Finance and Budget), Rodolphe Adada (Mines and Hydrocarbons) and Pierre Moussa (Planning). A Minister from Oyo village who is not a direct relative is Christian Gilbert Bembet (Information and Telecommunications).

While presidential family members in the government include Antoine N'Dinga Oba (Foreign Affairs and Cooperation), Benoit Moundele N'Golo (Public Works and Construction, Gabriele Oba Apounou (Youth and Sports), and Presidential Cabinet Director, Aime-Emmanuel Yoka,[54] this does not preclude the fact that family members in the government are either competent or Marxist.[55]

A long time ago the Pool region was the threat to the Ngouabi regime. As the country's first two Presidents, Abbé Fulbert Youlou and Alphonse Massamba-Debat, came from the Pool, it is clear that the Laris and Kongo peoples remain less enthusiastic about the current political system. To control this region, Sassou Nguesso has appointed Combo Matsiona and Ganga Zanzou to the Politburo.

The Omnipotence of the Movement of 22

There is no doubt that Ngouabi had destroyed the M22's reputation. A long time ago the politicians who used to belong to the group of M22 were regarded as 'gauchistes'. Thus, they lost control over the Party. They had been defeated while Ngouabi's friend had full control, many years ago, of the whole society.

This situation has been reversed. Since the appointment of Sassou Nguesso at the head of the Party and the State as well, he has allied himself with M22 at the expense of the pro-Soviet group in the Party at least temporarily. Nothing of this has happened to Ngouabi. Many of today's political observers believe that the M22 is, so far, omnipotent.

Already there are complaints from the youth organisation about the M22's influence. It is clear that Oba Apounou, a youth organisation leader and Sassou Nguesso's nephew, is in bitter personal rivalry with Camille Bongou, the Secretary General of the P.C.T. and leader of the influential M22 group. As a counter-balance, the youth organisation (Oba Apounou, N'Gakala,

Eba Sylvain, Camara Dekamo, N'Gatse Paul) does not carry weight. What is sure is that the M22 group has increased its power, and the trend will continue. As a good strategist Sassou Nguesso will certainly reduce the influence of the M22. Partly because the M22 is the possible threat to his position – partly because it is no longer possible for Sassou Nguesso to share collegial leadership with the M22.

At the PCT congress which will be held in July 1989, changes are predicted. Camille Bongou will be replaced as the second political figure of the PCT. While Oba Apounou is becoming a member of the political bureau of the central committee, Ganga Zanzou, President of the National Assembly, is likely to be replaced by Health Minister Bernard Combo Matsiona. Ange Edouard Poungui, Prime Minister, could be replaced by finance minister Pierre Moussa or by trade, small and medium enterprises minister, Poaty-Souchoulaty. Auxence Ickonga is expected to return to Government, possibly as finance minister. Yoka Aime Emmanuel should return to the Government, with either the planning of Finance portfolio. As we can see in the Congo, 'on prend les mêmes et on recommence'.

What kind of conclusion do we come to after 29 years of independence?

Without drawing a conclusion on the political transformations in the Congo, one may say that there were always conflicts instigated by tribal or ideological struggle. Before Sassou Nguesso came to power, the Congolese Labour Party itself was torn by useless quarrels between moderates and radicals. It took some years for Sassou Nguesso to reconstruct a united party that could run the nation effectively.

In such a way, Nguesso will continue enjoying popular support. Subsequently he could run the country for a long time. The possibilities of the palace revolution are limited – because the army still remains loyal to Nguesso. [56]

Also all radical allies in 1979 have been purged from position of real power and influence.

Tchystere and Tsiba, have been removed from all party functions. At the same time, Nzé lost his position as a Politburo member as well as Foreign Minister, while Sylvain Goma was removed both from the Politburo and as Prime Minister. Gouelo-Ndele, a long-standing friend of Ngouabi and the big boss of State Security, was sacked. Ndala Ernest, one of the prominent radicals in the country since the mid-1960s was condemned to death, accused, of plotting a bombing campaign. Committee central stability will determine how much longer Sassou Nguesso remains in power.

The more worrying aspect comes from Sassou Nguesso's approval of the I.M.F.'s programme for the Congo. For many, the I.M.F.'s structural adjustment plan is 'anti-social'. He is also reproached for his privatization programme. The state enterprises are perishing faster than before, or they are being legally liquidated, usually by the blatant and simply scandalous sale of the enterprises to cronies of certain leaders. [57]

After 26 years of the revolution, the Congolese society is divided into three distinct political generations: the first, the old, is related to all members controlling the Party and government in Ngouabi's name, committed to his interpretation of what Marxist-Leninism should be in a hot, tropical climate. They include those who belonged to the M22. Their common denominator is the 'anti-imperialist struggle'. This old generation have something akin to a charmed life. They may fall out of favour from time to time, but they can usually count on being rehabilitated.

The new generation wants more openness in the Congo's political life and is pragmatic like Sassou Nguesso himself. Their common denominator is being both Marxists and technicians. They are frank, realistic, hearty about the situation in the Congo. They are few in the Party, so, the opportunity for them to speed up reforms is very limited.

The third generation is what we call the 'eternal generation' who see things in terms of tribes. Some among them support the Congolese Labour Party, some are against it, some are indifferent.

The Nature of the Congolese Labour Party (P.C.T.)

In order to be able to throw some light on the nature of the P.C.T., we must first remind ourselves that the Party was a response to the failure of the National Revolution Movement (mouvement national de la revolution) to build up a Socialist country. As Kouka Kampo, a Congolese political theorist and well-known philosopher said, quite rightly, the birth of the Congolese Labour Party was a response to an objective and pressing need for social development. [58] This brings us to the idea according to which the Party did not appear like the sunrise in a given period. Beyond Kouka Kampo's rosy rhetoric the main point is that the birth of the P.C.T is not related to a voluntarist act, but is the outcome of the political economy and social circumstances. The Party by its structure and its objectives is a vanguard party. No difference should exist between the Party and the workers, so long as the Party reflects the interest of the workers. Needless to say, the Party had made big strides in its quest for international recognition as a Marxist-Leninist party.

In spite of the fact that the Party is a vanguard one, the capacity of the Congolese Labour Party members to place the interests of the nation above their own interest is still questioned. That is why the Party is facing enormous purges.

The Party and Purges

Since the creation of the Party in 1969, one can say that its task was not made any easier by its own members. From time to time the Party is engaged in continuous purges against 'alien elements'. This means that in the context of the Congo, the best way to accelerate the revolution is to get rid of 'alien elements'. For example, Kouka Kampo shows why it is useful to use purges. He argues compellingly that the Party is strengthening itself by the method of purges. [59] In fact, in Kouka Kampo's view, the purges are the basis of a significant revitalization of the P.C.T. It is this tie that seems to us harder to break. Congolese leaders' political ups and downs, of course, from 1963 to now, have been dominated by purges, rehabilitation and renewed purges. Noumazalaye's fate, during the *putsch* of the M22 movement, was the familiar one of humiliation: arrested, sentenced to death, released, he was once again arrested, released after the assassination of Ngouabi in 1977 and appointed as a minister in the early 1980s. Ndala Graille, the second Politburo member in 1970, was purged and sentenced to death after the 1972 *putsch*, and again released by Sassou and again arrested on grounds of complicity in the 1982 bombings and sentenced to death again in 1986. Bongou Camille was arrested and purged during the 1972 *putsch*, rehabilitated by Sassou Nguesso in 1979 and he became the second Politburo member until 1987. Henri Lopes was purged in 1975 and was appointed as a Minister of Finance in 1977 by Yhombi. Nzé Pierre became a Politburo member in 1973, purged in 1975, he was sent to the countryside in 1977, rehabilitated by Sassou Nguesso in 1979 and became again a Politburo member and Foreign Minister, but was again purged in November 1986. Yhombi Opango, by 1972 was a Politburo member and Chief of Staff of the army. Very soon he was offered an unexpected honorific position of Inspector General of the Armed Forces. With the radicalization of 1975 he was no longer a Central Committee member. After Ngouabi's death he became a member of the military committee and President of the Republic. Even Sassou Nguesso, regarded as a member of the original P.C.T. Politburo in 1969, had to attract Ngouabi's anger as he was accused of being a behind-the-scenes manipulator of the 1971 students' disorders. In these matters, he was briefly purged from the Politburo following the Diawara affair in 1972 but came back as one of the five members of the Special Revolutionary General Staff (état major spécial révolutionaire) and the first Minister of Defence in Ngouabi's régime. From that period, he was also considered to be the régime's number two.

Table 5: The Social composition of the P.C.T., 1984	
	percentage
Workers	13.90
Peasants	17.25
White-collar employees	31.68
Intellectuals	25.00
Soldiers	1.42
N.C.O.s	5.45
Officers	5.30

Source: *Zeme Congres* p. 31

Table 6: P.C.T. membership, 1971–86					
1971	*1975*	*1982*	*1984*	*1986*	*1990*
227	1,427	7,000	8,865	9,000+	10,000

Source: *Thompson and Adolf* (1980, p. 188, GICA, 1984, 1987).

Notes

1. Salvatore Foderaro: *Independent Africa* (Colin Smythe Ltd., England, 1976, p. 75).

2. See Michael Lofchie: 'The Uganda Coup – Class Action by the Military' *The Journal of Modern African Studies* (10.I, 1972, p. 19).

3. Robert M. Price: 'A theoretical approach to military rule in New States: Reference group theory and the Ghanaian case *World Politics* (Vol. 23, April 1971, pp. 339–430).

4. Samuel Decalo: *Coups and Army Rule in Africa* (Newhaven and London, Yale University Press, 1976).

5. Samuel P. Huntington: *Political Order in Changing Societies* (Newhaven, Conn., Yale University Press, 1968).

6. See Claude E. Welch *J.R., Soldier and State in Africa* (Evanston, III North-Western University Press, 1970).

7. J. Gus Liebenow: 'The Military Factor in African Politics' *A Twenty-five Year Perspective*

in African Independence Edited by Gwendolen M. Carter and Patrick O. Mears (Indiana University Press, 1985).

8. Marien Ngouabi: 'Scientific Socialism in Africa, Congo Problems, Views and Experience' *World Marxist Review* (May No. 5, Vol. 18, 1975).

9. Ngouabi Major Marien – A Kouyou, born at Ombele in 1938. He was admitted in 1960 to a military school in Strasbourg, and from there went to St. Cure, graduating in 1962 with the rank of Second Lieutenant. On his return to the Congo, he was assigned to the Pointe-Noire as Second-in-Command. In 1963 he was given charge of the newly-created paratroop corps at Brazzaville, with the rank of Captain. During this period, he was said to have become an avid reader of Marxist literature. His demotion in June 1966 and his arrest in July 1968 led, respectively, to an army mutiny and the military take-over of the government. Successively he became Commander-in-Chief of the armed forces, founder and Chairman of the P.C.T., and the President of the Republic. After several attempts on his life, Ngouabi was assassinated on 18th March 1977.

10. African Communist, 1976, 'New Way in Congo People's Republic'.

11. J. Gus Liebenow *The Military Factor in African Politics: a Twenty-five Year Perspective* (Op. cit.)

12. See Damuel Decalo: *Coups and Army Rule in Africa* (Op. cit. p. 159).

13. Major Mouzabakani Felix: Born at Brazzaville in 1932 into an influential Lari family. A professional army officer, he was named deputy Chief of Staff after Youlou's eclipse. He was condemned to death by the Massamba-Debat regime, but was released and named Minister of the Interior by Ngouabi. He was removed from the government because of the lack of Socialist convictions.

14. See *West Africa*, March 8th, 1969, 'Congo-Brazzaville reactionaries arrested'.

15. See Africa Contemporary Record 1972–73.

16. See *Le Monde* du 19 Avril, 1975.

17. See *West Africa* 30th April 1973, 'Congo rebel leaders shot'. See also *West Africa* 10th March 1972, 'Congo-Brazzaville *putsch* suppressed'. See also *West Africa* 7th May 1973, 'Ngouabi on Diawara'. *West Africa* 20th March 1973, 'Congo – Anti-guerilla operations'.

18. During the night preceding the *coup d'état* of February 22nd, 1972 Diawara, Matounda-Ndolo and their followers kidnapped three of Ngouabi's loyal friends, Foreign Minister Henri Lopes, Vice President Moudileno Massengo and Pierre Nzé of the Political Bureau.

19. See *West Africa*, 26 February 1973, 'Congo: police in plot'.

20. West Africa 29th October, 1973, 'Congo: Army reshuffle'.
    Note: Diawara's guerilla activities had led inadvertently to the death of Chief Adjutant Moussa Eta, who was killed while looking for Ange Diawara by Sergeant Ntala who was later accused of collaborating with imperialism.
    Note: About army reshuffle, it was reported that 'Captain Mathias Ferret had been named as Commander of the Brazzaville Military Region'.

21. See *Jeune Afrique* No. 6015 Juillet 1972, 'Congo: le spectre de Diawara'.

22. Explanation given by Christoff Moukoueke, the Party's propaganda secretary to Vladimire Shundayer in the *African Communist* 1976.

23. See *Le Monde* du 23 Mars 1976, 'Le Congo de la radicalisation, une auto-critique courageuse.'

24. Ibid.

25. See 'la declaration du 12 Decembre 1975'.

26. Speculations about the resignation of Henri Lopes and the appointment of a military Prime Minister reached the following comment: 'In the context of the Angola crisis it is better to have a military Prime Minister to put the government on war, then Henri Lopes who had been too pro-French'.

27. A special revolutionary general staff was established to take charge of preparing an extraordinary party congress. The members of the new regulationary general staff were President Ngouabi, Major Goma (Prime Minister), J.P. Thystere Tchichay (in charge of party headquarters, organization and administration), Major Denis Sassou Nguesso (Defence and Security) and Jean Pierre N'Gombé (propaganda, education and information).

28. Among the militants purged by a movement of radicalization were the former minister, Christophe Moukouéké, who became Secretary General of Brazzaville University, Anatole Kondo, the C.S.E. Secretary General, Charles Madzou and Ekamba Elombé, Permanent Secretary of C.S.E. Also purged was Jean Jules Okabando, the leader of U.J.S.C.

29. See *Los Angeles Times*, 29 July 1977, 'Congo finds it can't exist on Marxism', by David Lamb.

30. See *Jeune Afrique*, Paris, 1 Mars 1978.

31. See *Le Monde* du Avril 1977.

32. See *African Contemporary Report*, 77–78, B.552.

33. See Sassou Nguesso, in *Oraison funèbre*.

34. A communiqué broadcast over Brazzaville Radio on 3rd April named the military committee as follows: Head of State, President Joachim Yhombi Opango, First Vice President, Sassou Nguesso; Second Vice-President, Louis Sylvain N'Goma; other members, Jean Michel Ebacka, Nicholas Okongo, Francois Xavier Katali, Pascal Bima, Martin Mbia, Florent Siba, Raymond N'Gollo, Pierre Anga.

35. Joachim Yhombi Opango, was born in Owando, Northern Congo, in 1933. He served in the French army from July 1957 until independence in 1960. After studies at the Strasbourg Military School, he graduated as Second Lieutenant from St. Cyr. Returning to Congo in 1962, he joined the Congolese army and was named Commander of the First Congolese Company, a post he held until August 1963. In 1965, he was sent as military attaché to the Congolese Embassy in Moscow, where he served from July 1965 to July 1968. Recalled by Ngouabi, he was appointed to lead the elite Para-Commando Battalion. He became Army Chief of Staff in November 1965, Inspector General of the Armed Forces in 1973.

36. It is well known that Pierre Nzé and Christophe Moukouéké were sent to the Southern and Northern villages, where they used to live with poor farmers.

37. West Africa, 14th November 1977, 'Self-criticism in the Congo'.

38. In reference to the debate broadcast on television celebrating the third anniversary of the declaration of 12 December 1975.

39. In the motion for the March congress, the P.C.T. politicians made certain specific claims: Opango had bought a solid gold bed from Gabon for 17 million C.F.A. francs of Development Aid given by Algeria to the Congo for the construction of a water tower. One newspaper claimed that much of this was used to lay out Yhombi's estate at Mpila which includes a zoological park. It is said that this cost 200,000 C.F.A. francs daily to maintain.

40. Niccolo Machiavelli: *The Prince* Edited by Quentin Skinner and Russell Price (Cambridge University Press, 1988, p. 68).

41. Bokamba-Yamgouma, a General Secretary of the Congolese Trade Union Federation, was a courageous militant who denounced publicly the spectre of envelopes received by certain members of the Party.

42. In the interval of the Congress which is the supreme organ of the Congolese Labour Party (P.C.T.) the Central Committee is the centre of power. Its members meet three times a year. The executive organ of the Party is the Political Bureau.

43. See Michael Radu and Keith Somerville: 'The Congo in Politics, Economy and Society' *Marxist Regimes* Ed. Printer (Publishers Limited, London 1981, p. 179).

44. Sassou Nguesso, 27 at the time of his take-over, a parachute regiment officer, like Ngouabi and Yhombi, had been active in politics since Ngouabi's take-over in 1968, and was a member of the National Council of the Revolution and P.C.T. Politburo until December 1971, with responsibility for co-ordination with the masses. He was promoted to major in 1975 and was named Defence Minister the same year following the fall of the Henri Lopes government. At the same time he became one of four members of the special revolutionary general staff with responsibility for the permanent committee for the Army, Defence and Security. He became first Vice Chairman of the Military Committee and was promoted to Colonel.

45. See the Fundamental Law promulgated by General Yhombi Opango on 5th April 1977, shortly after he succeeded Major Marien Ngouabi in a manner contrary to the constitution then in force.

46. Theophile Obenga, Congolese Foreign Minister who paid two days of visit in Paris, insisted that the real reason for Yhombi's resignation was that the P.C.T. wanted to return to 'the spirit of modesty and revolutionary commitment', *Le Monde*, Paris, 3 March 1979. See also, *New African*, April 1979, 'Congo-militants take over'. See also, the *African Communist*, 1979, 'Congo: Denis Sassou Nguesso takes over'.

47. African Confidential, February 28th, 1979, 'Congo-Brazzaville – palace coup'. The palace revolution, engineered during the Central Committee meeting brought to power a group of pro-Soviet and pro-Cuban army officers, with civilian Marxist-Leninist advisers. It is said that Sassou Nguesso is an admirer of Fidel Castro and Angolan President, Agostinho Neto. He was supposed to call back two left-wingers, Ambroise Noumazalaye and NDalla Graille to take over key posts in the administration. France,

Belgium and the U.S.A. are upset by these events for they fear an additional source of destabilisation in adjacent Zaïre.

48. African Confidential, 7th September 1983, 'Congo: the revolution goes west'.

49. Katali should have been removed from the Political Bureau but as he was an influential man, it was impossible for Sassou Nguesso to extinguish him politically in a simple, direct attack. Sassou Nguesso had to undermine Katali's position gradually to the point that he had concentrated the security issues in his hands.

50. Daniel Abibi, brilliant lecturer of mathematics, was Chancellor of Ngouabi University, then Minister of Secondary and Higher Education. He wrote Sassou Nguesso's speech of the extraordinary congress of the Party in 1979. Abibi's 'Marxism' is heavily tinged with radical African nationalism, a mix which is said to be close to the President Nguesso's own outlook. Abibi is likely to be elected to the P.C.T. Politbureau at the next Party congress which will be held in July 1989.

51. See *African Contemporary Record* 1984–85, B133.

52. Jean Pierre Tchystere-Tchicaya was the P.C.T. Politburo's official ideologist and the guardian of Marxist purity. A Vili from the Pionte-Noire region, he controls Education and Ideology in the Party and had rallied numerous southern cadres behind Sassou Nguesso. He is closely tied to former Prime Minister Pascal Lissouba. A member of the former royal family of the Loango kingdom, Tchicaya is trying to cobble together a coalition from his own Kouilou region with the neigbouring Niari.

53. Colonel Louis Sylvain N'Goma, Prime Minister of the Congo. Born in Pointe-Noire on 28th June 1941, and passed out of France's St. Cyr. Ngouabi's faithful ally, he was appointed Chief of Staff. Promoted to Major in 1973, N'Goma's dedication to the revolution and loyalty to Ngouabi brought about his appointment to the revolutionary general staff in December 1975 and also as Ngouabi's Prime Minister.

54. See *Africa Confidential* of 17th October 1984, 'Congo: Ideology is out'.

55. Before Sassou Nguesso became President, Oba Apanou was an active militant of the Youth Organization and a second personality of this organization. It boils down to the same for Antoine NDinga Oba who was Minister in Yhombi's government, while Aimé Emmanuel Yoka was Vice President Moudileno Massengo's Cabinet Director. Moundele N'Golo was for a long time an active militant of Congolese Labour Party – considered as a close friend of Diawara. He just married Diawara' widow.

56. See *Le Monde*, Dimanche 26–Lundi 27 Fevrier 1989 'Congo; le dixième anniversaire de l'arrive du pouvior du Général Sassou Nguesso, la révolution assagie'.

57. See *New African*, November 1988. 'An extraordinary document has been published by the Congo's unique political party, the Marxist P.C.T. which criticized its leader President Sassou Nguesso and accuses him of selling out of capitalists.'

58. Kouka-Kampo, Head of Department, Standing Secretariat of the Central Committee, Congolese Labour Party, in debate about vanguards in the making on the development of revolutionary parties in the socialist oriented countries: *World Marxist Review* Volume 29. No. 1, January 1986.

59. Ibid.

The Economic Change

ONGOLESE ECONOMIC CHANGE since the revolution is both an interesting and important case study in which we can explore the interaction
of ideology, policy and practice in the process of policy formulation and
implementation, The relationship between ideology and policy means that
economic and technical decisions will be primarily political decisions which
will be linked to a centralized Socialist ideology. No discussion of Africa's
economic problems is complete without a reference to the mismanagement
of public resources by African governments. Instead of placing the blame
wholly and primarily on external factors, we should take account of internal
factors. This approach will help us to understand the economic change of
the Congo.

The Economy of the Congo and the Massamba-Debat Era (1963–68)

In the early sixties, there was no political economy, as the responsibilities
for economic activities from the rise to the fall of Youlou were in the hands
of private sectors. The régime of Youlou was characterized by many economic
and social problems: chronic unemployment, a trade deficit and the absence
of tangible development. After the overthrow of Youlou, the Congo's basic
problem was not how to run an economy, but the lack of capital. The new
team led by Massamba-Debat and his Prime Minister, Pascal Lissouba,
obviously inherited a difficult economic situation. There was virtually no
industry, with the result that, for example, tinned orange juice was imported
although oranges grow in abundance.

The high costs of administration took three-quarters of the annual
budget. Most roads were bad and often impassable in the rainy season.
Travelling from Brazzaville to Pointe-Noire may take anything up to
three days. Inadequate infrastructure and transport was a constraint on
food marketing and discouraged agricultural production. Other problems
include inadequate skilled manpower to administer the State. Hospitals
and other vital services were poorly staffed Such were the conditions in
the Congo soon after independence. In 1964, to reverse the deteriorated

75

economic and social conditions, Massamba-Debat enunciated a new Socialist-oriented economic policy in which the State would play a dominant role. The State would dominate the entire process of economic growth.

A New Era of Economic Development (After 1963)

To facilitate the proposed changes, the new government made a start first in cutting administrative costs. In this respect, the President's salary was halved; deputies got less, and had to continue with their professions. More significantly, the civil service was reduced by almost a quarter; of the 9000 administrative posts, 2000 were abolished.

In the five-year plan (1964–68), the government envisaged total expenditure of 50.700 million francs C.F.A. and an annual investment rate equivalent to about 30% of G.N.P. of this. Forty percent of planned expenditure was to be allocated to industrial production, some 15% to primary production, about 20% to economic infrastructure and nearly 25% to social overhead infrastructure. [1]

In order to implement the first five-year plan, loans and credits were required. An Israeli group had assisted in the cotton industry while West Germany provided aid for timber production. In the educational sector, Unesco contributed towards secondary schooling. [2]

The new régime made an effort to redress the economic and social inequalities existing between the urban centres and the rest of the country.

The most impressive aspect of Congolese economy during the Massamba-Debat period is the rapidity and pace of industrialization in the country; it was considered to be fourth in French-speaking Africa.

For instance, the Congolese sugar industry, with a capacity of 100,000 tons, was the largest in that group, and was able to export to other African countries. In addition, there were other important industrial units, a cigarette factory in Betou, a fish-flour factory and glassworks. At the same time, the extension of the oil-palm plants in Fort Rousset (now Owando), Mokouango, and Etoro produced 3000 tons in each centre. With a cement factory, the Congo absorbed the relative number of unemployed.

Explanations

The analysis of the Congo's relative economic progress leads to the search for explanations. Roughly, there are two factors: first, there is no doubt that the adopted strategies had successfully and speedily spread development to the interior of the Congo. Second, the bureaucrats were usually conscientious in their activities. Without good strategies combined with the good will of the bureaucracy, it was difficult to see how the Congo could have achieved relative economic and social progress. The factors cited as explanations played some role, but not as effective causes.

Rural Sector

Between 1964–1968 the Congolese leaders approached the rural sector from two angles, ideological and productive, aiming to produce enough to feed the villages and towns, and to create enough jobs to be able to absorb the surplus manpower that could not be accommodated by the public sector.

Table 7: Labour and Employment in Select Years 1964–83 (in thousands)

	1964		1973		1977		1983	
	Number	%	Number	%	Number	%	Number	%
Agriculture	202	74	226	48	215	45	193	34
Government			22	5	41	8		
Public Enterprise	70	26	22	5	29	6	42	7
Private Urban			198	42	197	41	332	59
Total Labour Force	272	100	468	100	482	100	567	100

Source: *Bulletin quotidien de l'ACI*, May 5th 1966, *Ministère du Plan, Recensement agricole 1972–73, Census annuaire statistique*, 1982.

As indicated in the above table, agriculture provided jobs for 74% of the labour force during the period of 1964. Export of agricultural products constituted the main domestic resources (but declined in value by more than 20% between 1964–66).

The launching of the first five-year plan (1964-68) helped the agricultural system to break out of a period of semi-stagnation, which had characterized the Youlou regime. The Congo was self-sufficient in cassava, sugar, maize, fruits and vegetables. About 35 to 40 per cent of the families were living in frugal but satisfactory conditions. Often the families had two meals per day.

Table 8: Agricultural Production (in tons)

	1964	1965	1966	1967
Groundnuts shelled	2,206	1,920	2,664	3,170
Groundnuts unshelled	2,206	1,920	2,664	3,170
Cocoa	842	911	1,140	1,534
Coffee	1,410	1,921	1,640	1,867
Maize	229	604	348	268
Paddy Rice	1,625	560	463	1,720
Palm Fruits	7,828	2,956	1,946	227
Tobacco	428	347	197	599
Palm almonds	4,037	3,198	3,383	3,372

Source; The economic commission for Africa's summary 1969

Table 9: Principal Exports (US/million)

	1964	1965	1966
Timber	18.7	17.8	19.2
Diamonds	19.7	19.8	15.2
Mineral Products	1.5	1.4	1.2
Petroleum	1.0	1.0	0.9
Palm oil	1.4	1.2	0.7
Total all items	47.3	41.1	37.2

Source; *Africa contemporary record* 1968–69

Compared to the economic situation left by Youlou Fulbert, it might be regarded as a success that Congo, with the ability and the determination of a new team, moved from bad to good The first five-year plan (1964–68), based upon on optimistic assumption of the influx of foreign assistance, did not materialize. At the end of the plan period in 1968, public sector investment had fallen far behind targets. The end of the plan also coincided with the change of the government in 1968. The new government, headed by President Marien Ngouabi, declared its intention to follow Scientific Socialism as a vehicle to economic development. Also, the government set aside the second five-year development plan (1970–74). [3]

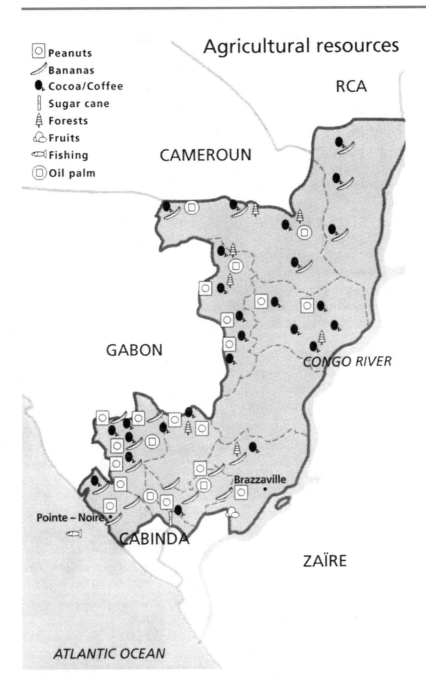

Agricultural resources

Legend:
- ⊡ Peanuts
- ⟋ Bananas
- ⬤ Cocoa/Coffee
- ⏐ Sugar cane
- ♠ Forests
- ⌂ Fruits
- ⊃ Fishing
- ⊙ Oil palm

RCA

CAMEROUN

GABON

CONGO RIVER

Brazzaville

Pointe – Noire

CABINDA

ZAÏRE

ATLANTIC OCEAN

The Economy on the Path of 'Scientific Socialism'

In the mid 1970s, it was well established that the new team led by Ngouabi had inherited an interesting economic situation, This was because the former government did well and left enough money. This appeared as an advantage. Over the period 1965–73, the average annual rate of increase of G.D.P. was 6.8% in real terms.[4] Is Scientific Socialism really the answer to Congo's economic problems? If the economy did not improve, it would be difficult to blame 'Scientific Socialism'. More importantly, it will be interesting to examine the action and role of policy makers.

As Ngouabi said: 'If nothing is going well, the fault is not with the Scientific Socialism, but with the lack of conscience of some leaders'. He added: 'The Party must run the State and that implies that we must appoint its members at the top of the State and all levels. We must only appoint hard-working, reliable, serious and efficient Marxist-Leninist members. Not those who give a bad impression of the Party.[5] Generally speaking, the practice of putting party members in most of the important government positions had damaged the efficiency of the administration.

The Economy and Patterns of Nationalization: New Policy 1970

By the end of the sixties, the role of the State was large and the volume of criticism of private enterprises reached unprecedented levels.

The choice of 'Scientific Socialism' implied that the State would intervene to decide how the economy would function. This meant that the government would try to influence events in one direction or another. Therefore, one cannot leave the crucial decisions to the free influence of market forces.

Under these conditions, nationalization seemed to the Congolese authorities the best thing to give a boost to the economy. All public services and transport systems were nationalized and more government control was introduced throughout the economy. Failure to run nationalized enterprises efficiently has struck a serious blow to the Congolese model of socialism. For example the Congolese sugar industry (la S.I.A. Congo), which is the main unit of production, has an annual deficit of 1 billion (Francs C.F.A.), while well managed, the same industry might provide 2 billion of net benefit.[6]

State enterprises encountered difficulties before the policy of nationalization. The sugar output reached 100,000 tons. A few years later, the output fell to 7,000 tons.[7] In the eighties, it reached the lowest level of 2,000 tons.

The low level production of groundnuts has impeded growth in the vegetable oil industry.[8] Similarly, the cement industry has declined.

Bureaucracy and Mismanagement

Relative decline of the economy was related to the mismanagement of state enterprise. Most politicians had no economic training and they were only interested in Socialism in words. Most of the factories which had shown outstanding performance in the early sixties produced even less a decade later. Some of them had gone to the wall. Bureaucracy has been the main cause of economic deterioration. The upper echelons of the civil service, along with politicians and the military, undermined 'Scientific Socialism'. They held a number of advantages, including relatively high salaries, easy access to public and private credit. At the same time, corruption was rife. These facts are not the subject of dispute.

To summarize: the nationalization of substantial parts of Congolese enterprises that occurred in 1970 was related to the idea that the public owners of resources were superior to market allocation. However, the experiment has proved costly to the Congolese economy. Over the period, growth has been low and the standard of living of people has progressively declined. In this matter, the government has to encounter difficulties to satisfy the high expectations of the rapidly growing mass of urban youth.

Deterioration of Agricultural Activities

Since the early 1970s, the advance in economic growth, characterized by the emergence of oil, was accompanied by the decline in agriculture. The structure of the economic production between 1965 and 1984 speaks for itself. In 1965 agriculture provided 19 per cent of the G.D.P., industry 19 per cent (manufacturing close to zero), and services 62 per cent; while in 1984 the same figures were 7, 60.6, and 33 per cent.[9]

The agricultural sector which represented the main source of employment (74% in 1960), declined to 36% in 1979–80. During the two years, according to national accounts data, agricultural exports amounted to only between 5% and 6% of total exports compared to 8% in 1960, and 12% in 1970.[10]

At the same time, the Congolese authorities continued to assert that agriculture was the top priority (la priorité des priorités). It sounds like a major contradiction, as agriculture represents an insignificant part of G.N.P.

(Gross National Product). According to Ngouabi, 'Ten years ago we didn't develop enough agricultural activities. It is really a contradiction. The trend has been rather to create state enterprises in order to resolve some problems of development, including those of unemployment. Thus, the agricultural sector has suffered from relative neglect.'[11] In the early 1970 years, cash crops (les cultures commerciales) as exports, were much less important than minerals or timber.

For this reason, the Congo was far from self-sufficient (auto-suffisance) in food. It is surprising to note that agricultural exports, which consist mainly of coffee, cocoa, sugar, palm kernels and tobacco, accounted for only 12% of total exports in 1970. This declined to 6% in 1974 and reached its lowest level of 1% in 1982. As agriculture represented the main source of monetary income to the rural population, it is obvious that agriculture's share of the nation's income has declined in recent years.

A Three-year Plan: Response to the Deterioration of Agriculture

To reach self-sufficiency in food (l'auto-suffisance alimentaire), the accent was placed on agriculture. Thus everywhere in the Congo you can read 'l'agriculture, priorité des priorities'. Thanks to the expansion of oil and potash, the government has been able to launch a three-year plan 1975–77 (le plan triennal). This represented a major chunk of the total investment of C.F.A.F., 76 billion.[12]

With this investment, the Congo would launch 'operation manioc' (or Fertilizer Programme), which should make the country self-sufficient in cassava, its staple food crop. At the same time, substantial increases in production of cotton, coffee, cocoa, tobacco and sugar are planned. The objective was to use oil and potash income to develop agriculture. It is clear that, after the boom of 1974, oil production declined dramatically during the following years, while the potash mine had to be closed in 1977 due to severe flooding.

With the collapse in petroleum production, the public sector salaries which took up half the budget,[13] the rate of unemployment, which continued growing, poor agriculture, the Congo henceforth condemned to import food including beef. The economic situation of the Congo during Ngouabi's period was a disappointment.

Table 10: Three-year plan (billions of C.F.A.F. and percentages) 1975–1977

	Planned Outlays	Percentages Allocations	
		Planned	Actual
Agriculture			
Forestry	11.6	15	3
Fishing			
Industry			
Mining	12.6	17	28
Economic			
Infrastructure	19.9	26	24
Services	31.9	42	43
Total	76.0	100	98
Financing			31
Domestic			69
Foreign			

Sources: Ministry of Planning 1975–77

In a period spanning little more than nine years Congo has witnessed a complete cycle in central government's policy. Central planning and State ownership have been adopted at the expense of private ownership and the market. As we have seen, the reasons for nationalization and its objectives have been many; but the overriding one was to use public ownership as a vehicle for economic development. The perception that the economic situation was slowing down and nationalized enterprises had failed, appeared to have been shared by all the political leaders, including Ngouabi himself. In response to the failure in the economy, the Party was obliged to move from nationalization to a mixed economy with a substantial public sector.

Explanations

The expansion of the public and semi-public enterprises was the key factor in deteriorating agriculture. The deterioration of the agricultural sector itself has also been the prime motive behind the mass exodus from rural areas to the cities, especially to Brazzaville and Pointe-Noire. With the educational system which provides higher school education only in the cities and their vicinity, students who would like to pursue higher education have had to go to the union centres to do so and to search for employment upon graduation. Poor roads: rural infrastructure in the form of trunk roads, and rural access roads are the sectors which have shown a decline from independence to now. Lack of access roads discourages the peasants from producing more than they consume. Even if progress has been made in this matter, much still remains to be done.

The Effects of Agricultural Change on Society

The agricultural decline brought with it two fundamental problems: first, the country had to import agricultural products to feed its population. The country was no longer able to grow all the food it needed. As a result, demand for imported goods has increased. This puts up the cost of food in the Congo. Second, oil dependence led to the greater neglect of the vital agriculture sector. Therefore, farm workers became underpaid in relation to workers with comparable skills in industry or civil servants. Observation tells us that the average wage of farm workers a month was regarded as being well below the poverty line for a man with a family to support.

In a country where agriculture was an important source of the exports needed to earn the revenue with which to purchase equipment and new materials for industrialization, stagnation in agriculture had direct effects on the progress of industry.

Can Yhombi Handle the Economic Situation? (1977)

When Yhombi took office as the fourth President of the Congo, he inherited difficult national problems: deficit budget, deficient infrastructure (roads, railways), poor agriculture and last but not least, a Central Committee of the Congolese Labour Party that surely intended getting its way on major issues.

The main concern, for instance, of the military committee was to pay the salaries of the workers. This seemed quite difficult as the revenues from oil and other agricultural products had declined.

For this reason, assistance was required from Gabon, the Ivory Coast and Algeria and from the oil states.[14] This led to a general impression that the economic situation was far from being improved and Yhombi Opango was not in a position to revitalize the economy. Not only was there little money, but the phenomenon of corruption was still incurable. A talented military man, Yhombi called first of all for discipline. What we call 'laissez-aller' was the characteristic of many state enterprises. It was widely felt that the only thing which would save the economy from collapse was to improve the situation of state enterprises and to reconsider agriculture as a 'major priority'.

The military committee was aware of the fact that there were no efficient officials (cadres competents) and the state enterprises suffered from ineffectiveness (inefficacité). [15] After two years in power, Yhombi failed to take corrective measures to improve the economic situation. The deterioration of the economy exacerbated the anger of the people. Everything was down (tout est par terre). As a matter of fact, it was an illusion to expect spectacular results.

The Transition to Oil Economy: Congo is Fuelled by Oil (1982)

Thanks to the oil boom euphoria in 1982, the Congo has become black Africa's fourth largest oil producer. It must be said that the whole economy was relying on oil.

Apparently, the Congolese government didn't play a positive role in using the total flow of funds from oil to improve the economy. The sectors which made a little progress were the construction (bâtiments) and public works (travaux publics). [16]

In referring to the role of oil in the economy, it should not be forgotten that oil accounted for nearly 80% of export earnings in 1982, raising the Congo's trade surplus from $16 million in 1978 to $250 million in 1982. [17] Oil has brought a rapid and massive influx of wealth into the hands of party leaders. Therefore an unfair imbalance between some leaders in the Party and the peasant majority was deepened.

Oil Economy and Obvious Failure

The Congo needed the oil revenue in order to implement its ambitious plan (1982–86). However, dependence on oil had a negative impact on the economic and social structure of the country to the point where it had created excessive expectations of future income based on unreliable estimates of the behaviour of the oil market. As Sassou Nguesso said himself to the P.C.T. meeting on 20th June 1985: 'Petroleum is constantly giving us unpleasant surprises' (le pétrole ne cesse de nous réserver de mauvaises surprises).

Congo's economy has been increasingly badly hit by the years of declining oil output. For instance, oil exports fell to $800 million in 1986 from $1 bn. in 1985. Also total oil production was down to 5.5m tonnes from 5.8m tonnes in 1985. [18]

The Outcome of the Oil's Failure

With the reduction in oil revenues, one can say that the Congo has to face a financial crunch. [19] For one thing, the lack of flow of capital pushes the country to revise its five-year plan (1982–1986) by reducing the volume of public investment, by adopting a three-year freeze for civil servants' salaries, and by renewing attempts to improve state sector enterprises, which continue to show a deficit (of C.F.A. 30 bn).

Then, as economic problems mounted, the Congo had to seek assistance from the I.M.F., which is largely controlled by the governments of the industrial countries. Thus a structural adjustment programme has been adopted. [20] Economic austerity, which presumes that belts must be tightened, will probably breed problems for Sassou Nguesso inside the Congolese Labour Party. As many are considered as orthodox party members, if anything more hardline than Sassou Nguesso himself.

Another outcome of the oil failure was the debt burden. As the public revenue was limited, the need for borrowing increased the amount of external debt. For instance, the debt service was set at $333 million for 1985, falling to $321 million in 1986. According to optimistic assumptions, the debt burden would weigh more heavily on the economy into the 1990s. Under such conditions, it seemed difficult for the government to attain its objectives.

The paradox is that even with the reduction in oil revenues, the Congolese élite continued its high profile. Congo was one of the rare African countries to increase significantly its consumption of up-market champagne in 1982. Luxurious villas in the capital are springing up like mushrooms. Congolese potentates are trying to insure against domestic troubles: luxury flat-buying abroad has switched from Paris to Brussels and Geneva. Summer holidaying in Europe is also *de rigeur* for the Congolese potentates. [22] The real problem now is how to revitalize the economy without relying on oil. There is only one solution: increase other exports.

After the Oil Era: Inevitable Reality, 1987

The decrease in world oil prices led the Congolese leaders to develop the other exports.

Turning to the other exports, efforts have been made. For instance, Congo's second export, timber, gained a boost from the International Finance Corporation (I.F.C.) and Banque Développement des Etats de l'Afrique Centrale (B.D.E.A.C.) for a $11m. five-year programme to double capacity at the Société Congolaise Industrielle du Bois (C.I.B.) from 59,000 cubic metres to 110,000 cubic metres and build a sawmill capable of producing 50,000 cubic metres of logs a year. Total timber production showed a significant increase to an estimated 251,000 cubic metres in 1984.

In addition, coffee and cocoa output rose in 1984 and investment increased in other agricultural sectors. France is backing a programme to expand tobacco production and exports. It is also funding a national seeds programme, while the British are rehabilitating oil palm plantations. Yet, with a lot of sacrifice, Congo can do better. For decades the country has shown a particular predisposition for economic progress: a lot of natural resources and a small population (so far 2 million – it is expected to reach 10 million in the year 2030).

Table 11: Population Growth and Projections

Population (millions)			Hypothetical size of stationary population (millions)	Assumed year of reaching net reproduction rate of n
1986	*1990*	*2000*		
2	2	3	10	2030

Source: *World Bank Report* 1988

Above all, Congo has one of the highest per capita incomes ($1,100) of tropical Africa, long since having escaped the category of least-advanced countries, or poor nations. The national wealth is abundant to provide a sound economic basis. To stimulate domestic production, there are two possible measures: for one thing, teach the young to like the land and not to move from the countryside to the urban centres.

Table 12: Urbanization

Urban Population				Percentage of urban population in large city
As percentage of total population		Average annual growth rate (per cent)		
1965	*1985*	*1965–80*	*1980–85*	*1960–1980*
35	40	3.5	3.6	7	56

Source: *World Bank Report* 1986

Then there is the responsibility of government to revitalize agriculture by increasing investment and the adoption of improved methods.

Despite its relatively good economic growth, the Congo has difficulty in creating jobs and revitalizing the state enterprises which are in financial difficulties. In addition, the world economic order imposes strict restraints on the shape of the domestic economy.

Table 13: Distribution of Gross Domestic Product (per cent)

Agriculture		Industry		Manufacturing		Services, etc.	
1965	*1986*	*1965*	*1986*	*1965*	*1986*	*1965*	*1986*
19	8	19	54	—	6	62	38

Source: *World Bank Report* 1988

Despite the priority of boosting production, there is a need for considerable investment in basic infrastructure like roads, railways and urban transport and amenities like electricity and water supply. Infrastructure has already shown signs of progress: for example, three new ferries assembled from French parts are now in operation between Brazzaville and Kinshassa. The realignment of the Congo Ocean Railway (C.F.C.O.) was completed in the summer of 1985 but the company now faces a rolling stock shortage and the prospect that the investment will be undermined once Gabon's Manganese ceases to use the line in Autumn 1987. France, West Germany and Canada have supplied locomotives and Britain some wagons. Congo has launched a national shipping line, la Congolaise de transport maritime (Cotram).

Aid and Austerity

By mid-1988, the economic situation was looking grim. The accumulated deficit of the state companies reached CFA 100 Bn, From that period, closures included Société de Transport de Loubomo, SONACEM, and société congolaise de meuble (SOCOME). These were followed by Société industrielle d'articles en papier (SIAP CONGO), cimenterie domaniale de Loutété (CIDOLOU), office congolais des matériaux de construction (OCMC) and office congolais des forêts (OCF). In response to this situation Canada had to cancel its debt in 1989, while other Paris club donors held talks on re-scheduling of some of the CFA 55Bn. During the same year, France announced a large number of loans totalling some FF268m for support for services to governments, departments, for infrastructure (rehabilitation of the office des postes et telecommunications, power production and distribution, port and railway maintenance) for rural and urban development of the forestry and wood industries. This included FF30m for the 1989-91 5000 ha expansion of eucalyptus plantations by Unité d'Afforestation Industrielle du Congo (UAIC)

External financing is playing an important role in the Congo's development strategy. In May 1989, the World Bank announced a $35m loan for road maintenance, a $25m loan for education, another $25m for urban development and a $15m IDA loan to strengthen agricultural services. The EC approved an ecu36m aid for integrated rural development in the Pool and Cuvette regions including agricultural and forestry development, water supplies and roads. The African Development Bank supported the IMF-backed 1987-88 structural adjustment programme with a $51.1m loan in September 1988.

Notes

1. See the Congo's first development plan. Ministry of Planning.

2. See *West Africa*, Saturday 15th August 1964, 'The other Congo'.

3. See *The World Bank Report 1966*, p. 184

4. See *Africa South of the Sahara 1987* Sixteenth edition (Europe Publications Limited, 1980, England, p. 387).

5. Marien Ngouabi: 'Vers la construction d'une societé socialiste en Afrique' *Présence Africaine* (Paris, 1975, p. 222).

6. See *Le Monde* du 30 Avril 1975, 'Congo: le socialism à petit pas'.

7. See *Le Monde* du 2 Novembre 1979, 'Le Congo après seize ans de révolution. Les beautés et les fantaisies du socialisme scientifique'.

8. Le Monde du 2 Janvier 1988 'Congo: le marxisme en question: "or noir" "or vert".'

9. See the *World Bank Report 1966*, p.184.

10. G. N'Guyen Tien Hung, Op. cit., p. 51.

11. Refer to Ngouabi's interview in *Le Monde* de Janvier 1975, 'l'URRS et la Chine sont parmi les meilleurs amis du Congo'.

12. Ministry of Planning, plan triennal 1975–77.

13. It is well known that the Congo has a huge bureaucracy. The number of civil servants increased from 3,300 in 1960 to 21,000 in 1972 and keep increasing up to day.

14. See *Le Figaro* of December 26th 1977, 'Congo: Un socialisme à l'Africain'.

15. Le Monde du 8 Avril 1977 'Le Colonel Yhombi Opango appelle l'armée à respecter l'ordre'.

16. Le Monde du 27 Août 1985, 'Le Congo s'efforce de redresser une situation économique alarmante'.

17. The Economist, July 2nd 1983, 'Congo's economy: low on energy, flush with oil'.

18. See *Africa Review*, 1988.

19. Africa Confidential 7th September 1983, 'Congo: yesterday's oil'.

20. The focus of I.M.F.'s economic adjustment measures include promoting growth of the non-oil productive sectors (especially agriculture), further development of the oil sector, and tighter management of public finances and debt servicing.

21. Africa events February 1986 'Sassou Nguesso: neither Marx nor Cardin' – Until recently the West's perception of Colonel Sassou Nguesso was that of a Marxist in the clothes of the French fashion designer Pierre Cardin but in the past few years that image has faded.

22. Africa Confidential 7th September 1983, Op. cit.

The Prospects for the Future

FROM THE FOREGOING, it is clearly shown that the one shape a country's economic trajectory never takes is a straight line. For the time being, the Congo, like most third-world countries, faces economic problems. No matter how the difficulties occurred, what is relevant is to find out a way of solving these issues.

Towards a Possible Solution

Despite its adjustment problems, chequered political history, and its uneasy balance between revolutionary fervour and private enterprise, the Congo is potentially a rich country. However, some important problems still remain.

The greatest threat to the Congo lies in the fact that it has the highest number of educated people in Africa. This will be strongly accentuated in the coming years. This will provide more problems to the tertiary sectors.

Another problem will be the struggle between the State, which is not able to provide enough jobs, and the school-leavers, who have difficulty in finding jobs. Efforts should be made to close the gap. So far, the public sector has been the greatest employer. Perhaps private sector and small business should play an active role. For this reason, nationale bourgeoisie might be encouraged and developed.

Self-sufficiency in Food and Constraints

Because of the deterioration of agriculture as already discussed, a policy of 'self-sufficiency in food' is a necessity, but this requires incentive measures. Self-sufficiency in food is linked to constraints. The first constraint is the lack of access to credit. This has reduced the efforts of farmers to improve the production of cash crops. We cannot know how deep is the desire of the authorities to solve this problem in the coming years. The second constraint is the state of roads. Lack of access roads discourages peasants from producing more than they consume. There are signs of progress in this matter, but some problems still remain, It is clearly underlined in the five-year plan (1982–86) that transport equipment and the extension of the roads system are given high priority. There are two possible scenarios to the transport problem: one priority is the establishment of repair facilities in the primary and secondary urban centres, for maintenance. Another is the training of technicians and mechanics, who will carry out the repair functions.

As long as self-sufficiency in food is not put into practice, Congo is going to spend more on food imports than in the past.

Table 14: Agriculture and Food			
Cereal Imports (Thousands of metric tons)		Food Aid in Cereals (Thousands of metric tons)	
1974	1986	1974/75	1985/86
34	104	2	2

Source: *World Bank* Op. Cit.

As indicated by the table above, the Congo has increased its agricultural imports. The real explanation lies in the lack of incentive measures to boost agriculture. It is said that the Congo used to feed itself.

In the plateaux region, especially in 'Enkou' just west of Djambala, Bernard Guillot came to the conclusion that there was enough food (alimentation suffisante). At any time he went there he noticed the farmers had groundnut crops four times, maize crops three times and cassava crops five times a year. [1]

One of the requirements of self-sufficiency in food is storage facilities (les facilités de stockage). Although there is no data, observations tell us a lack of storage facilities of all types constitutes a big constraint on the marketing of agricultural products. For example, it was observed at Pointe-Noire that the fishermen had to work all night so that they could land their catch very early in the morning; then buyers could obtain their supply early enough to take it to destinations inland before the fish deteriorated. Some crates of fish were seen left on the beach waiting for a vehicle to move them inland for sale. By the time the vehicles arrived to pick up the crates of fish, they would be perished. Such a loss could have been prevented by the construction of a small cold store near the beach.

Another threat in the coming years will be management. For many observers, the Congo has poor management. This is well known by the Congolese themselves. 'We have got the money all right', says a taxi driver, 'but what about the management?' Oil revenue, which constitutes an important part of the economy, is run so far by the government. In 1983, data has shown that grossly overmanned state corporations lost $80m. and swallowed 16% of the government's budget.[2] The lack of management has definite cultural roots. The Congolese are traditionally more politically-minded. The country was run by political figures and by bureaucrats, but neither are production-minded. This tends to make the Congo less productive.

If state enterprises want to survive, and sometimes to be efficient, leadership of a high order is the first priority. In the Congo, there are too few chief executives around with the right combination of leadership qualities to enable the companies to weather the storms ahead. It will be harder to succeed simply because the bureaucrats of the one-party system are opposing. It is worth remembering that Ngouabi ran up against difficulties when he called party members to combine firm ideology with know-how. Mismanagement of the Congolese leaders is still a touchy subject. It sounds like what we call 'a zone of silence'.

Another problem that still remains is corruption. Revolution cannot succeed with strong corruption. This has also added to the country's economic problems. The real fear is that by not doing their jobs well enough, the tax collectors and those who deal with money have affected the State's finance. A lot of fraud and irregularities are observed in the work of the collectors. The most common fraudulent practice implies paying taxes of a value less than what should be paid, and pocketing a bribe in return. The practice of 'madesu ya Bana'[3] is going up and up. The corruption is not limited to the tax collectors or customs officers, but hits the high state officials to the point of saying that 'the cancer of the corruption is the evil of the country'. How should the Congo avoid the corruption? Above all, the high state officials and important political personalities should set an example of national civic behaviour. So far there are no signs of change.

Table 15: Government current revenue

Taxes on Income Profit and Capital		Social Security Contributions		Domestic Taxes on Goods and Services		Taxes on International Trade and Transactions		Other Taxes	
1972	*1986*	*1972*	*1986*	*1972*	*1986*	*1972*	*1986*	*1972*	*1986*
19.4	—	0.0	—	40.3	—	26.5	—	6.3	—

Source: *World Bank Report* 1988

For the time being it is more a matter of mobilizing resources than expanding them. The country, a long time ago, was worried about domestic resources. How should government proceed? The government's effort in order to mobilize domestic resources should be concentrated on raising the share of tax revenue in G.D.P., improvement in the financial performance of public sector enterprises, and reduction of public expenditure.

At CFA 34.2Bn, customs receipts in 1987 were 16.2 per cent down in 1986, while other fiscal receipts dropped 18.3 per cent to CFA 46.2Bn. Standing at CFA 136.4Bn in 1987, as against CFA 227.9Bn the previous year, total receipts were down a massive 40.1 per cent, only covering salary bills and interest on the national debt with difficulty.

Government projections seem difficult to make – the target for the industrial sector is 4.5 per cent, for forestry 47 per cent. Excluding petrol, GDP is expected to grow by 2 per cent per year from 1990. The government foresees an annual growth of 2.9 per cent in oil exports with prices around $18 per barrel in 1992 and the dollar equivalent to CFA 300. A budgetary deficit of CFA 54Bn is foreseen for 1992. Growth of 4 per cent per year for the period 1989–92 is the government objective.

Congolese politics have been a cocktail of Marxist-Leninist ideological utterances, public pressure and deeply-rooted ethnic, regional and personal antagonisms It is not easy to master these forces. They will cause more difficulties in the future and the Congo must minimize these negative forces which hinder it. Yet there is still hope. When circumstances change, so should strategy. By giving top priority to 'Scientific Marxism', decision makers have lost touch with reality. The world is opening up and interdependence will be the key to success in the future. The division between Capitalist and Socialist societies is disappearing. Not the societies themselves, but the argument. The conception of an interdependent system is cutting across the old view of the world consisting of the simple Socialism/Capitalism dichotomies. The new world that is emerging is far more complex and does not lend itself to the simple identification of the previous two groups.

Foreign Policy

Two important distinctions should be made concerning the evolution of the Congo's diplomacy. The first stage is linked to Youlou's regime. During 1960, there was no doubt that the Congo had privileged relations with Western countries, especially France, the Congo's former colonizer. In addition, the Congo became an active member in the conservative 'Moronvia Group'. Youlou's diplomacy was characterised by 'anti-communism'.

Three years later, after the Congolese revolution of 1963, the official anti-communism stance was reversed. Faced with Imperialist provocations and attacks, the Congo chose deliberately to develop ties with Communist countries for security reasons. It also expressed its support for the progressive liberation movements in Africa. So Massamba-Debat's diplomacy was marked by the denunciation of Imperialism.

What about African issues? The choice of Socialist orientation did not prevent the Congo from following a policy of 'friendship and good neighbourliness'. Whatever the choice of other African states, the Congo has maintained its relations with them.

In this part, the Congo's foreign policy will be examined with African states, Western Europe and Communist states. We will analyse the main reasons for the current pattern of relations. Economically, the Congo has a lot to gain in developing its relations with Western countries. For example, France still remains a country which trades considerably with the Congo. See Table below.

With other states of Africa, especially Zaire or Gabon, strategic reasons figure largely. As the Congo was the first country which decided on 'Scientific Socialism', there was a danger that imperialist powers could use its neighbours to destabilize its revolution. In addition, the Congo's economy relies relatively on its neighbours.

Table 16: Changes in Congo's volume of trade with main partners 1985–6

Country	1985	1986	% change
France			
Imports	1,107	968	-4.8
Exports	2,355	1,823	-22.3
United States			
Imports	6,145.6	397.9	-38.4
Exports	19.4	10.1	-47.9
United Kingdom			
Imports	2.8	2.4	-14.3
Exports	21.5	9.2	-57.2

Source: *QER, April,* 1987

Considering its relations with the Soviet block and other Communist states, ties are related to ideology, with the reference to the principle of International Solidarity.[4]

Diplomatic Relations with African States

Congolese relations with African states might be interpreted in two ways: first of all, it is clear that Congo has followed a policy of 'friendship and good neighbourliness'. Secondly, because of its Marxist orientation, Congo has shown sympathy with the so called revolutionary African States.

Looking at its relations with its neighbours, difficulties only appeared with Zaire. The main cause of hostility between the two countries is an ideological difference. A long time ago Congo accused Zaire of supporting Youlists – while Zaire strongly criticized Congo for supporting the anti-Mobutu 'progressives'. With the Angolan conflict, in which Congo and Zaire supported opposite sides, relations got worse and worse. Despite enormous tensions between Congo and Zaire, efforts have been made by the two sides to improve relations. In February 1976 Ngouabi succeeded in reconciling President Mobutu and the M.P.L.A. leader, Agostinho Neto.

Since Sassou Nguesso came to power, relations between the two countries are better – as Sassou Nguesso has softened his position and is tactful and, beyond all, respects Mobutu, Zaire considers Congo like its own suburb. The Congo's relations with Zaire reached the lowest level in April 1989, following reciprocal expulsions from those countries of Congolese and Zairean nationals who were alleged to be residing illegally in their host country. In order to resolve this situation, Sassou Nguesso made an official visit to Kinshassa.

Congolese relations with Cameroon have been affected by the Congo's support for Marxist opponents of Ahmadou Ahidjo in the early days of the Massamba-Debat regime. Now relations are better, if not close.

Relations with Central African Republic were fairly poor during the régime of Bokassa. This was due to the fact that Bangui was unable to pay its transport bills within the Central African community (Chad, Congo, Cameroon, Central Africa). Difficulties arose when Congo had to support Abel Gouba's front patriotique d'Oubangui parti du travail against Bokassa.[5]

Congolese relations with Gabon have always been good and stable, since Ngouabi and Bongo liked each other. In addition, Gabon guaranteed to send a share of Moamga's manganese exports via Pointe-Noire even after the completion of the Transgabonaise railway. There is no doubt that economic interests have overcome ideological differences.

The best that can be said is that relations with the four states of French Equatorial Africa and Congo have been good throughout post-independence. The four countries and Cameroon shared the same currency, The African Financial Community Franc.

Apart from its relations based on the principle of 'good friendship and neighbourliness', Congo has expressed its sympathy with revolutionary African states. Ngouabi defined the Congo's position as one of non-alignment, qualified to mean alignment on the side of just causes and therefore anti-imperialist. In referring to this principle, the Congo has supported the liberation movements of Namibia and Zimbabwe. It also pledged support and aid to the Saharouis struggle in Western Sahara. Ties have been reinforced with Algeria, Mozambique, Benin, Libya and Egypt.

Diplomatic Relations and Western States

During the Youlou régime, Congo had established good relationships with Western countries. With strong French economic interest in the Congo, relations between the two countries were important. As Youlou's political view was anti-Communist, his régime expressed its sympathy with the United States. Therefore, Youlou paid a visit there in 1962.

The revolution of 1963 introduced change in relations with Western countries. Hence the militants considered the United States as the head of world Imperialism. At the same time, French Imperialism was denounced, but in 1967, President Massamba-Debat decided to improve ties with France, whatever their political differences. On the contrary, relations with Great Britain had been broken in December 1965 over the Rhodesian affair. Relations with the United States reached a low level.

In 1973, Congo needed aid from the United States. For this reason, Congolese authorities began making discreet overtures to Washington, using the good offices of President Mobutu of Zaire. But Ngouabi's support for M.P.L.A. and the use of Congolese territory by the Cuban combat forces, destroyed any interest Washington may have had in reopening diplomatic ties with Congo. In 1977, only a month after Marien Ngouabi's assassination, Ybombi made efforts in order to reopen the American Embassy in the Congo. It is said that Theophile Obengo was a Congolese negotiator in Bonn where the agreement on resuming relations has been signed.

So far, relations with the United States are not as bad as they were, but the Congolese Labour Party had condemned the American raid on Libya as well as the American policy in Nicaragua. Sassou Nguesso whose election as Chairman of the O.A.U. in 1986–1987 was in recognition of his active intervention in African affairs, notably in the search for a solution to the conflict in Chad, paid a working visit to the USA in October 1987. He praised the US Congress decision on sanctions against South Africa and urged the political diplomatic and economic isolation of South Africa; he criticized the US policy of linkage between Namibian independence and the withdrawal of Cuban troops from Angola. He didn't meet President Reagan during the visit However, he was received by Vice-President Bush.

In talks with the French Prime Minister, Jacques Chirac, prior to the Franco-African Summit of November 1986, Sassou Nguesso protested at the visit to France of Unita's leader, Jonas Savimbi, and the South African President, Peter Botha. Sassou Nguesso's diplomatic success has been his role as mediator in negotiations between Angola, Cuba, South Africa and the USA, which resulted in the signing, in December 1988, of the Brazzaville accord, regarding the withdrawal of Cuban troops from Angola and the question of Namibian independence.

Diplomatic Relations with East

Diplomatic relations with the East had begun in the year 1964. For the Congolese authorities the Soviet Union and China are Congo's closest allies – not only for ideological reasons, but for the aid provided.[6] True, Congolese relations with the Communist states have consistently been characterized by attempts to maintain an intricate balance between their ideological, military and political influence and the continuation of economic ties with the West.

Up to now, Congolese relations with the Communist world continue as before, with the gradual development of closer party and government ties to the Soviet block and warm relations with China. Both the Soviet Union and the Congo celebrated the fifth anniversary of the signing of the Congo-Soviet Union Treaty of Friendship and Co-operation.

Economically, the Soviet Union and China have supported or financed some projects. The large Soviet-built Cosmos hotel and nightclub was completed in 1968 while China built the radio transmitter near Brazzaville to provide radio links with Congolese embassies in Paris, Peking and Cairo.

To summarize: Congolese relations with the West, especially France, could be interpreted as 'Congo's search for economic security.' An absence of friction with the West, particularly France, on which Congo was and is so dependent for aid, constitutes the base of economic revitalization. On the contrary, by the beginning of 1964, imperialist military attack on the Congo's revolution had aroused the sympathy of Eastern countries, particularly the Soviet Union's. In my view, the Congo's foreign relations display a contradiction between ideological aspects and economic means. It is clear that ideological differences are secondary, since the Congo needs capital and financial assistance to realize its ambitious development plans.

The end of the Cold War brought in Congo a democracy based on the rule of law, a market economy with predominantly private ownership. President Mitterand announced at the sixteenth Franco-African Summit, held in La Baule in 1990, that France would help African countries which are moving towards democratic change. At the same time the World Bank with the International Monetary Fund (IMF) insisted on economic liberalization and democracy as the price of their assistance. As a result of this pressure, Mathieu Kerekou of Benin, Denis Sassou Ngresso in the Congo, Gmassingbe Eyadema in Togo and Kenneth Kaunda in Zambia accepted the principal of the national conference used for democratic political change and free, fair presidential and parliamentary elections.

Notes

1. Bernard Guillot: 'La terre Enkou (Congo) *Atlas des Structures Agraires au sud de Sahara* (Paris, Mouton, 1973, p. 102).

2. See *The Economist*, July 2, 1983

3. 'Madesu ya Bana' is a Lingala word which means a reward in money of collectors or customs officers when they fail to tax the goods in referring to its own value. Often it is an arrangement between collectors and taxpayers.

4. See Jean Pierre N'Gombé: 'Towards a new upsurge of the revolutionary process' *World Marxist Review* 'Vol. 20, No. 9, September 1977'.

5. See Michael Radu and Keith Somerville: Op. cit. p. 218.

6. See Ngouabi's interview in the French newspaper *le Monde* du 12 Janvier 1975, 'L'U.R.S.S. et la Chine sont les meilleurs amis du Congo'.

Brazzaville in the Civil War: An Ugly Fight over a Pretty City

CONGOLESE SHED THEIR BLOOD from the very beginning of June 1997. History records that the civil war began on June 5, 1997 with President Lissouba's decision to send troops to attack the heavily guarded Brazzaville residence of former President Sassou Nguesso. A closer examination of events preceding the civil war strongly suggests that enmity had begun between Lissouba and Sassou Nguesso in late September 1992. At the root of the problem was the very large and very deep question of power sharing. In August 1992, Pascal Lissouba, the leader of the UPADS, won 36% and 61% of the votes respectively in two rounds of presidential elections, defeating both Bernard Kolelas, the leader of the MCCDI, and Sassou Nguesso. In the wake of the second round, Congolese Labour Party (PCT) members became involved in Pascal Lissouba's campaign Sassou Nguesso strongly and enthusiastically recommended that those of his supporters who were ready to rip up their vote cards shift to Pascal Lissouba. At the same time, an agreement on a common programme of government was signed between Sassou Nguesso and Lissouba. According to Moungounga Nguila,[1] after Sassou Nguesso found that he could not win the election because he was behind Lissouba and Kolelas, Sassou Nguesso decided to make an agreement with Lissouba.

In September of 1992, Maurice Stephane Bongho-Nouarra was appointed as Prime Minister to form a coalition based on a UPADS-PCT parliamentary alliance. As a consequence of the dispute over the number of ministerial portfolios to share, the PCT broke the alliance. Thus, PCT ministers such as Mvouba Isidore[2] resigned while his peers Lefouoba and Henri Ockemba remained cabinet members. By underestimating the weight of PCT voters on his victory, President Lissouba was going to pay a high price for his misjudgment. Throughout early September 1992, just back from England where I was a research scholar at Cambridge University, I worked with Christophe Moukoueke,[3] the Secretary General of UPADS. He had been my mathematics teacher in secondary school. I repeatedly warned him of the responsibility of Lissouba for preserving this agreement. Without abandoning or diminishing my claim to the respect of the agreement, I told Kikounga Ngot, who was in touch with Lissouba, to persuade him to avoid breaking the agreement by making concessions.

The PCT tactics during 1993 consisted of forming the alliance with the Union pour le Renouveau Democratique (URD) and winning a vote of no confidence in the government while trying to create a political crisis which would seriously jeopardize Lissouba's term. The URD-PCT alliance, which had a majority of seats in parliament, had expressed the right to form a new cabinet. Lissouba found that he was faced with a choice between accepting the new alliance to constitute a new cabinet or dissolving the National Assembly. It had been reported that Lissouba was negotiating with the leaders of the URD-PCT alliance in order to work cordially with this alliance. Even more important was the choice of Jean Pierre Tchystere Tchicaya, Gabriel Bokilo or Jean Martin Mbemba as Prime Minister. So strong was the opposition from the 'Mouvance presidentielle' leaders such as Yhombi, Moukoueke and Ganao. It did not come as a surprise when Lissouba dissolved the National Assembly and announced that the new legislative elections would be held in 1993. That had to be tough news for the leaders of the URD-PCT alliance. This dissolution raised its own problems. Therefore, Bernard Kolelas, the MCCDI leader and chairman of the URD-PCT, urged his supporters to launch a protest campaign of civil disobedience. Despite attempts by Lissouba to prevent bloodshed, in the second half of 1993 clashes between Lissouba's supporters and Kolelas' supporters became more serious in the Bakongo Quarter. That led to the emergence of the phenomenon of militias. Each political group organized its own militia at the expense of the Army. In order to secure its power, UPADS created the 'Aubevillois' militia. A similar militia called 'Ninjas' was affiliated with the MCCDI. To defuse this political crisis, the Chief of Staff of the armed forces, Jean Marie Michel Mokoko,[4] intervened to demand that the two sides form a transitional government pending the holding of the new parliamentary elections. Mokoko could have seized power at this point as he had the backing of Bernard Kolelas. Then Lissouba appointed his friend Antoine Dacosta as Prime Minister.

There were symptoms of the coming civil war prior to the presidential elections which were held in July, 1997. While pursuing power through elections, Congolese politicians kept their military options open by forming militias. They were armed with heavy and light machine guns. The 'Cobras' militia was created in 1993 by General Pierre Oba and Colonel Michel Ngakala. 'Zoulous' or 'Aubervillois' belong to Lissouba's three areas, Niari, Bouenza and Lekoumou. This militia was created by Colonels Nguembo and Dascosta. The militia called 'Ninjas', affiliated with Kolelas, was created by Colonel Philippe Bikinkita. As you can see, nothing could stop Lissouba, Kolelas and Sassou from calling upon their militias to fight if their interests were undermined.

In the meantime, attention was increasingly focused on the presidential election scheduled for July 1997. Opposition parties called for the establishment of Republican institutions, more balanced access to the media, and the establishment of an independent electoral commission. Ganao, who replaced Yhombi as Prime Minister, announced that his government was going to organize the next presidential election. Bernard Kolelas, considered so far as Sassou Nguesso's ally, had decided to run for President without the consent of the URD-PCT alliance. Sassou Nguesso, unwilling to face the possible humiliation of another defeat after his first presidential loss, considered that Kolelas' decision to run as a power arrangement between Lissouba and Kolelas. Further, MCCDI members joined Lissouba's government, while PCT members through FDU refused to participate. By encouraging his régime and MCCDI members to move towards each other, Lissouba had created the basis for political election at the expense of Sassou Nguesso. Mathematically speaking, no potential candidate would win without making a coalition. After all, history had shown that a coalition between Jacques Opangault and Kikounga Ngot led to the success of Opangault. Perhaps a coalition between Sassou Nguesso and Kolelas through URD-PCT was likely to lead to the success of Sassou Nguesso if he had been the only candidate of this coalition. Based on currently available information, it can be stated with certainty that Yhombi, who had never accepted that Sassou Nguesso was the only leader in the North of Congo (RDD has more than six members of parliament), was appointed as Lissouba's campaign manager in order to turn Northern voters' opinions against Sassou Nguesso, since the vote in Congo appeared to be tribal. This pre-election struggle was going to lead to civil war. It did not come as a surprise when, in May 1997, fighting erupted in the Northern towns of Owando and Oyo between supporters of Sassou Nguesso and Yhombi Opango.

The Turning Point

It is my view that civil war was hidden behind political appearances or pretexts. Whether Lissouba hung on to the power or Sassou wanted to return to power by any means, the truth is that both loved power. On June 5, 1997, with Lissouba's term running out and presidential elections scheduled, Lissouba sparked the war by sending troops to disarm Sassou Nguesso's Cobras. Why had he decided to take this action at the last moment? Mberi Martin, co-chairman of UPADS, considered that Lissouba would risk a civil war in which he was not going to win. He distanced himself from Lissouba. This event precipitated the immediate response of Sassou Nguesso's militia. Foreign observers in the Congo suggest that the Cobras were a strong organization and strategically shrewd. According to foreign observers, Sassou Nguesso could have seized power on June 8. There were indications that the Cobras were well prepared to fight and were confident that sooner or later Sassou Nguesso would return to power. Bernard Kolelas did not mince his words. [5] According to him, during the URD-PCT coalition, Sassou Nguesso wanted to plot a coup and to overthrow Lissouba, but Kolelas had always refused. As the situation was getting worse, the two sides were asked to Libreville to negotiate under the auspices of President Bongo. In the negotiations in Libreville (Gabon), neither side was completely honest. Given the reciprocal distrust that had existed for so long, perhaps they were unable to be honest. Every round of talks ended in deadlock, and both sides resumed fighting as a way of venting their frustration.

The uncertainty in the capital of Congo was exacerbated by two factors: Lissouba as President established a Constitutional Council, which, in turn, extended the end of his presidential mandate to postpone elections. In addition, Mayor Bernard Kolelas – considered thus far as a mediator at the national level – had rallied Lissouba's camp. He was appointed as Prime Minister in September. Kolelas had kept his own militia, the 'Ninjas,' neutral since June and his coalition with Lissouba represented a serious threat to Sassou Nguesso. It was agreed to resume talks between Lissouba and Sassou Nguesso in Libreville. It was a moment of extraordinary hope. These talks might help the Congolese end of the civil war and stop devastating the pretty city which was the capital of French Equatorial Africa. Unfortunately, Lissouba refused to go to Libreville, where his peers were waiting for him. He went to Kinshassa to seek the support of Desiré Kabila, while Sassou Nguesso participated at the meeting in Libreville.

On October 12, Sassou Nguesso launched a fresh offensive. After three days of heavy fighting for Brazzaville, Sassou Nguesso's supporters claimed control over the city. The best that can be said is that if it hadn't been for the Angolan intervention, which had brought troops, armoured vehicles and war planes into the war on Sassou Nguesso's side, the civil war would have dragged on much longer than it did. The United States recognized Sassou Nguesso' military victory. However, they showed concern about Angola's military activity in the region. The Angolans had now been permitted to pass two international borders to take out governments they didn't like. After Kabila seized power and drove Mobutu into exile in Morocco, where he died, Lissouba stepped into Mobutu's shoes. Angolan troops intervened because the Atlantic port of Pointe Noire became a major supply point. Both Lissouba and Sassou Nguesso embraced a civil war in which an estimated 10,000 people died, in order to stay in power or to gain power. They both care more about power than they do about the people. Sassou Nguesso, who initiated democracy in 1991 under international pressure and left power without bloodshed in 1992, did not trust Lissouba and could not accept Lissouba as the organizor of elections which, in Sassou Nguesso's eyes, would not be fair. Ever since Sassou Nguesso was ousted from his position, he and his followers have been seeking to get him reinstalled, one way or another.

The End of the Civil War and the Fall of President Lissouba

When Lissouba was elected in 1992,[6] many Congolese were euphoric. His election offered relief from the sometimes anti-democratic, three-decade rule of the single party. The government's economic and social recovery plan (PARESCO) was launched in order to bring about social and economic progress, which was seriously impeded by problems connected with the size of external debt. As a result, the Congo's structural adjustment programme was supported in 1994 by a one-year standby agreement backed by the IMF, and economic recovery credit from the World Bank, debt reduction by the PARIS club and other credits. The government succeeded in bringing the oil share contract to a level of 32%. At the same time, the Cuvette West region was created and the number of civil servants was reduced. But the euphoria has gone since he has disappointed those who voted for him by engaging in two civil wars during his term, despite his attempts to avoid bloodshed. Opposition politicians accused Lissouba of political and ethnic favouritism and he dismissed several high-ranking officers that Northerners

The Congo's Ten Regions

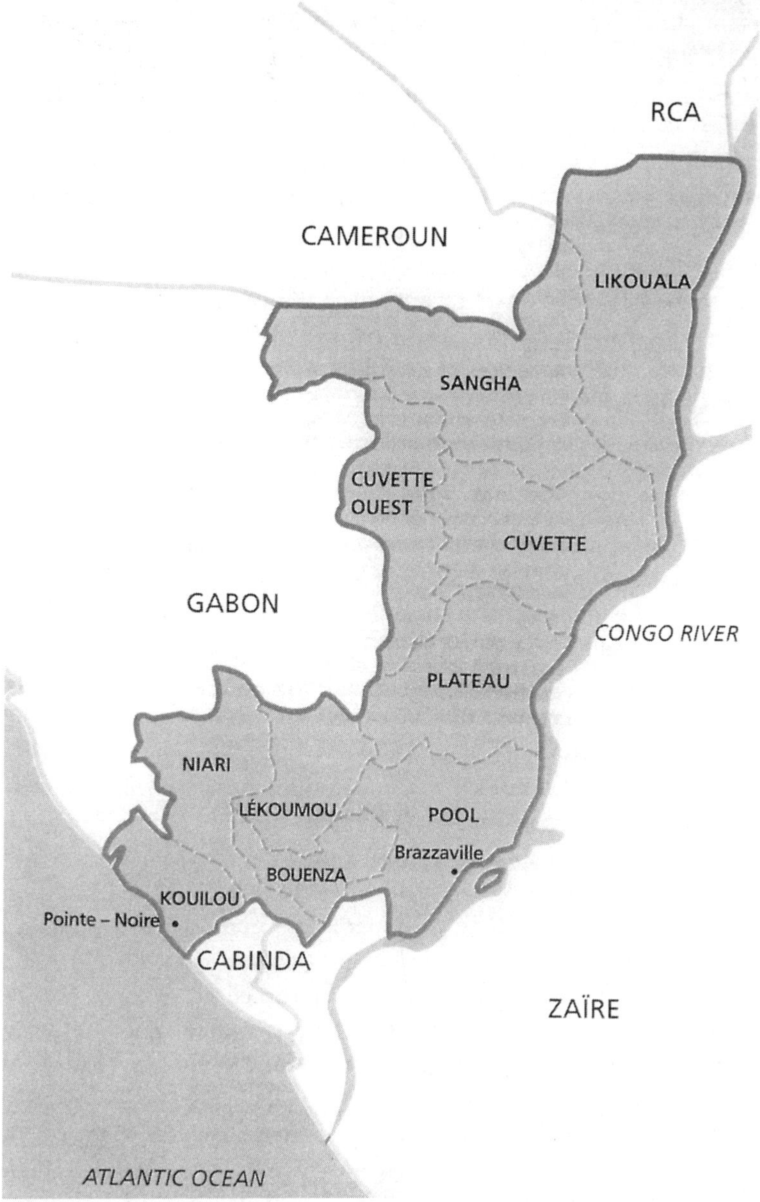
RCA
CAMEROUN
LIKOUALA
SANGHA
CUVETTE OUEST
CUVETTE
GABON
CONGO RIVER
PLATEAU
NIARI
LÉKOUMOU
POOL
Brazzaville
BOUENZA
KOUILOU
Pointe – Noire
CABINDA
ZAÏRE
ATLANTIC OCEAN

had installed during the Sassou Nguesso period. In democracy, it is not the party that usually rewards the President, but the voters. After his military defeat, he left the country with his close associates (Moungounga, Tamba-Tamba and Munari) from fear of certain death if he fell into the hands of Sassou Nguesso's forces. At the same time, he told the French station by telephone from an undisclosed location that 'I can only regard myself as President, since I have not seen in front of me my successor, elected democratically as I was.' This unrealistic statement led to the view that Lissouba forgot that there was a civil war and that the objective of each side had been to win the war and to seize power. That is why, after his military victory, Sassou Nguesso had decided to reward the warriors. On October 20, Lissouba had been granted asylum in Burkinafaso, while his Prime Minister Kolelas had gone into exile on the Ivory Coast. They both continued to recognize themselves as President and Prime Minister and chief of government in exile.

On October 25, Sassou Nguesso was sworn in as President after winning the power through war. In a speech at the Parliamentary Palace, Sassou Nguesso claimed victory over 'the old demons of discord and barbarism' and promised 'a new start, one of true reconciliation and national solidarity.' Despite his call for national reconciliation, Sassou Nguesso showed no desire to reconcile with Lissouba or with Lissouba's ally, Kolelas, saying that both men would be sought to face charges of genocide and crimes against humanity. A 75-member national transitional council was appointed to steer the country towards elections and to oversee its reconstruction. Sassou Nguesso's close associates (Lekoundzou, Mvouba, Pierre Oba, Dron Matthias and Bitsindou) occupied the most important positions. Unlikely Paul Kaya, considered as a rival of Lissouba, became number one for government and later he resigned.

By the end of October, Lissouba paid a visit to Washington. I met him at the airport and we stayed for two hours at his hotel. I had two things on my plate. My first question to him was why he sent troops to surround Sassou Nguesso's residence. I also asked why he turned down the Libreville meeting. Lissouba candidly explained that Sassou Nguesso put himself in that position. 'I could not go to Libreville because everything had been decided in advance.'

During his second trip, Lissouba came with Kolelas. After a news conference, I chatted with Kolelas and entreated him to do something about the rampage of violence that had erupted in Brazzaville since June 1997. He promised me there would be no more violence. He added that 'our purpose is to restore democracy in Congo.' A few days into December 1998, sadly, militias close to Kolelas harassed government troops. At the same time, Kolelas told the French station by telephone that his militias controlled the capital.

The truth is, the government troops seem as strong as ever. The war is over, but we will have to be realistic about everything else. The post-war goal is to move towards reconciliation, which requires change, a breaking of the cycle of conflict and the reconstruction of the devastated, though formerly pretty, city of Brazzaville, once one of Africa's more attractive and comfortable capitals, now a shattered ruin. Reconciliation is the key to overcoming Congo's economic and political problems and to avoiding stirring up ethnic divisions. The most basic misconception is that Congolese politicians, whether of the government or of the opposition, are learning that military solutions to problems are better than political solutions. The civil war in the Congo was about power, regardless of what might have been its precipitating causes. For them, peaceful solutions through concession and compromise are considered as weak solutions.

The experience of civil war in the Congo suggests a number of lessons: a poorly prepared election scheduled in July 1997 was a major factor in escalating the warfare. In reviewing the civil war in the Congo, great care should be taken in the use of the sweeping label 'ethnic conflict.' The lack of power-sharing is one reason for the civil war. Power-sharing usually works best when it is embraced by moderate political leaders who show imagination and flexibility in addressing inter-ethnic problems. Will the Millennium bring Sassou Nguesso, as a winner of the civil war, to preach national unity, ethnic harmony, and national reconciliation with Lissouba, Kolelas, and Moungounga? The senseless killing cannot continue. The murder of the civilian population and other barbaric acts such as rape should convince everyone that violence leads to no solution.

Political Organization

Coordination des partis indépendants: Brazzaville; f. 1997 as and alliance of 25 parties to contest presidential elections; Chair MBIKI DENA NITELANIO.

Forces démocratiques unies (FDU): Brazzaville; f. 1994 as an alliance of six political parties; Leader Gen. DENIS SASSOU-NGUESSO; Deputy Leader PIERRE NZE.

Convention pour l'alternative démocratique: Leader ALFRED OPIMBA.

Parti congolais du travail (PCT): Brazzaville; telex 5335; f.1969; sole legal political party 1969–90; socialist orientation; Pres.Gen. DENIS SASSOU-NGUESSO; Sec.-Gen AMBROISE NOUMAZALAY.

Parti libéral républicain: Leader NICEPHORE FYLA.

Union national pour la démocratie et le progrès (UNDP): f. 1990; Leader PIERRE NZE.

Union patriotique pour la réconstruction nationale: Leader MATHIAS DZON.

Union pour le renouveau nationale: Leader GABRIEL BOKILO.

Front uni des républicains congolais (FURC): f. 1994, regd 1995; promotes national development on a non-ethnic and non-regional basis; Chair. RAYMOND TIMOTHEE MAKITA.

Mouvance présidentielle: Brazzaville; f. 1992 as alliance of c. 80 political parties supporting Lissouba's candidature for presidency; Leader JACQUES-JOACHIM YHOMBI-OPANGO.

Union pour la démocratie et la république-Mouinda (UDR-Mouinda): f. 1992; Leader ANDRE MILONGO.

Union des forces démocratiques (UFD): Leader DAVID CHARLES GANAO.

Union panafricaine pour la démocratie sociale (UPADS): Pres. PASCAL LISSOUBA; Sec.-Gen. CHRISTOPHE MOUKOUEKE.

Mouvement africain pour la réconstruction sociale: Leader JEAN ITADI.

Mouvement pour l'unité et la réconstruction: f. 1997 as an alliance of three political parties; mems:

Mouvement pour la démocratie et la solidarité (MDS): Pres. PAUL KAYA.

Rassemblement pour la démocratie et le progrès social (RDPS): f. 1990; Pres. JEAN-PIERRE THYSTÈRE-TCHICAYA; Sec.-Gen. JEAN-FELIX DEMBA TELO.

Union pour la République (UR): Brazzaville; f. 1995 by breakaway faction of UPADS; Leader BENJAMIN BOUNKOULOU.

Mouvement patriotique du Congo (MPC): Paris, France.

Mouvement pour la réconciliation congolaise: Paris, France; f. 1996; Leader Gen. JEAN-MARIE MICHEL MOKOKO.

Parti africain des pauvres: f. 1996: Leader ANGELE BANDOU.

Parti congolais pour la réconstruction (PCR): Brazzaville.

Parti libéral congolais: f. 1990: Gen. Dec. MARCEL MAKON.

Parti du renouvellement et du progrès: Leader HENRI MARCEL DOUMANGUELE.

Parti social-démocrate congolais (PSDC): f. 1990; Pres. CLEMENT MIERASSA.

Parti du travail: f. 1991; Leader Dr AUGUSTE MAYANZA.

Parti pour l'unité, le travail et le progrès (PUTP): f. 1995 by defectors from the MCDDI; Leader DIDIER SENGHA.

Programe national de la jeunesse unie: f. 1996; Chair. LUDOVIC MIYOUNA.

Rassemblement pour la démocratie et le développement (RDD): f. 1990; advocates a mixed economy; Chair. SATURININ OKABE.

Rassemblement démocratique et populaire du Congo: Leader JEAN-MARIE TASSOUA.

Rassemblement pour la République et la démocratie (RRD): f. 1996; Leader Maj.-Gen. RAYMOND DAMASSE NGOLLO.

Union du centre: Leader OKANA MPAN.

Union pour la démocratie congolaise (UDC): f. 1989; advocates economic liberalization; Chair. FELIX MAKOSSO.

Union pour la démocratie et le progrès social (UDPS): f. 1994 by merger of the Union pour le développement et le progrès social and the parti populaire pour la démocratie sociale et la défense de la République; Leader JEAN-MICHEL BOUKAMBA-YAUNGOUMA.

Union patriotique pour la démocratie et le progrès: Sec.-Gen. CELESTIN NKOUA.

Union pour le progrès: Pres. JEAN-MARTIN M BEMBA.

Union pour le progrès du peuple congolais: f. 1991; advocates democracy and national unity; Leader ALPHONSE NBIHOULA.

Union pour le progrès social et la démocratie (UPSD): Brazzaville; f. 1991; Pres. ANGE-EDOUARD POUNGUI.

Union pour le remouveau démocratique (URD): f. 1992 as an alliance of seven political parties; Chair. BERNARD KOLELAS; prin. mems:

Mouvement congolais pour la démocratie et le développment intégral (MCDDI): Brazzaville; F. 1990; mainly Kongo support; Leader BERNARD KOLELAS.

Rassemblement pour la démocratie et le progrès social (RDPS): see under Mouvement pour l'unité et la réconstruction.

Table 17: SÉNAT*

Speaker: AUGUSTIN POIGNET

General Election, 26 July 1992*

Party	Seats
UPADS	23
MCDDI	13
RDD	8
RDPS	5
PCT	3
UDR	1
Independents	7
Total	60

* On 6 October 1996 elections were held for 23 of the seats in the Senate. The 'Presidential Group' of parties won 12 of the seats, retaining its majority, while opposition organizations took 10 seats and one seat was secured by an independent candidate.

Table 18: ASSEMBLÉE NATIONALE*

Speaker: ANDRÉ MILONGO

General Election, 2 May 1993 and 3 October 1993*

Party	Seats
UPADS	47
MCDDI	28
PCT	15
RDPS	10
RDD	6
UFD	3
Other parties	14
Independents	2
Total	125

*In January 1994 an independent electoral committee annulled the results in eight constituencies where there was found to be evidence of electoral fraud; three of the seats were held by supporters of the Government, and the remaining five by opposition members. At by-elections in seven of the constituencies, which took place in early 1995, three seats were won by the PCT, two by the MCDDI and two by the UPADS.

Notes

1. Moungounga Nguila was an influential finance minister in Lissouba's government and a founder of PCT, but he was never associated with the mismanagement of PCT.

2. Mvouba Isidore was Sassou Nguesso's rising star and FDU spokesman during the June 1997 civil war. He was later appointed as chief of Sassou Nguesso's cabinet

3. Christophe Moukoueke is a former member of the Central Committee of PCT and Secretary General of UPADS. He is considered number two in the party after Lissouba

4. Jean Marie Michel Mokoko was the chief of staff of the armed forces who handled the transitional government in 1991 with success and is considered as a well-respected military man.

5. Bernard Kolelas see *Conference News*, The Centre for Strategic and International Studies, Washington DC, 6 October 1998. prior to his appointment as Prime Minister, Kolelas served as the Mayor of Congo's capital city Brazzaville. Kolelas has been actively involved in the struggle for democracy in the Republic of Congo for almost 50 years.

6. In August 1992, Pascal Lissouba became the first democratically-elected President of the Republic of Congo, Lissouba held the Presidency until October 1997 when he was overthrown by militia led by former President Denis Sassou-Nguesso, following a four-month civil war. Lissouba competed for the position of transitional Prime Minister, losing by a small margin to Andre Milongo. One year later, he defeated Milongo and former President Denis Sassou-Nguesso to become President of the Comgo.

Learning From its Own Mistakes

EVEN IF EXAMINED through the most optimistic eyes, the Congo still remains a country in a state of flux. Today, there is apparent political stability. It was not always so. During the first decade of independence in 1960, the country faced many coups, political assassinations and executions.

Geographically divided into two parts, the South more rich than the North, ethnic tensions continue to destroy the possibilities of economic take-off. The strategy of 'auto-centre auto-dynamique', adopted to enhance the chances of development, was a failure. A blind admiration for 'Scientific Marxism' coupled with dogmatism led the country to the policy of nationalization. This was not so easy for a country with limited familiarity with 'management'.

Factories were under Congolese Labour Party members' supervision, but they were not technicians, engineers or scientists. While the country was considerably rich in agricultural products, concentration on oil production had been the cause of neglecting the agriculture sector. Subsequently, the Congo had to import food in order to meet its needs. Financially, as the commodities prices fell, the Congo was not able itself to finance the economy. Trying to mobilize Western aid sounds like a dilemma. Some Congolese Labour Party militants are convinced that Western aid will increase external dependence. 'Scientific Marxist-Leninism' is not viewed favourably by potential aids donors. In which direction then is it best to develop the economy? The civil servants did not really want to collect taxes or any customs duties for the state. Proportionally, much went into their pockets. As there were no good incentive measures, the goal of 'self-sufficiency in food' is still unquestioned. Even if the roads have shown signs of some social progress, the main difficulties are not over.

In addition, the gap between Party members, who have a lot of advantages and privileges, and the people who are eternally poor, is going up. The principle of the Party, according to which 'everything for people only for people' (tout pour le peuple, rien que pour le peuple) is hollow. With the vulnerability of an economy which is not able to create more jobs; with

10,000 bureaucrats of the party who refuse to change this reality; with the personal conflict of leaders; the way to speed up is in the hands of a new generation of politicians. who combine what Ngouabi himself required: know-how and non-dogmatic Marxism.

By a process of elimination, a new generation, more realistic than the old, will take over. The scenario for take-over is not hard to imagine. Despite Sassou Nguesso's good will and the pragmatism he upholds in placing national economic self-interest above ideology, if the economic situation doesn't show any changes and there are demonstrations because people are not satisfied, and if there is no adhesion inside the Party to his desire to develop ties with Western countries (The Soviet Union and the Chinese are now open to the rest of the world; why shouldn't the Congo be the same?), obviously Sassou Nguesso will call a new generation to implement a policy of success. As the reality gains ground from the ideology, the old guard, by a process of elimination will lose its positions.

This book leads to one conclusion: there is hope. It would be wrong to use pessimistic language as the country faces formidable problems. The itinerary of this book, both in space and time, covers more than two decades and is intended to throw light on the future. In fact this book has been written to show the Congolese officials how to turn failures into successes. That is undoubtedly lesson No.1. Since the Congo has adopted the road of Socialism, Chinese and Soviet Union relations have been reinforced at the expense of Western Imperialism, especially of France. What is now clear is that this was not a good strategy. It was stressed that the Congo has chosen a Socialist orientation and that foreign companies should nationalize, giving the state control of the economy. There is no doubt that the state must play a vital role in the economy.

Lacking an economic base and management know-how, nationalized enterprises were faced with formidable economic difficulties. Lenin's words, addressed to economic managers of the young Soviet Republic in the difficult years when it had to enlist foreign capital and grant concessions to help build up the Socialist economy, must be applied to the Congo. Lenin said at that time, 'You will have capitalists beside you, including foreign capitalists, concessionaries and lease-holders. They will squeeze profits out of you amounting to a hundred per cent; they will enrich themselves, operating alongside of you. Let them. Meanwhile you will learn from them the business of running the economy.' This might be lesson No.2.

The one-party system at the beginning has spent much time on individual disputes instead of concentrating on the people's interests. As a result, instability was the main drawback of the country. It was always 'l'éternel commencement'. The State, which is at the centre of things, must be stable. This would be lesson No.3.

More attention must be paid to pragmatism. Aid from Eastern European Countries, especially the Soviet Union, has not been adequate to meet Congolese needs. Thus there is nothing wrong with co-operating with the West. This should not mean that the Congo turns its back on Marxist ideology. If the Soviet Union, China and Vietnam enjoy co-operating now with the West, why shouldn't the Congo do the same? It is essential for the Congolese Labour Party members to understand that what counts is the improvement in the living standard of people. Pragmatism is lesson No.4. Sassou Nguesso, whose pragmatism is a part of his nature, has understood that it is vital to place economic realities above ideology. Do the Congolese Labour Party's members agree with him? That is another story.

With a sound economic future, provided it develops its agriculture, the Congo will have no problems in feeding its population of two million. But food deficits caused by a rural exodus, relatively poor infrastructure and the lack of incentive measures to encourage farmers, has increased its dependency on food imports; relegating the humble yam, cassava and other traditional produce, to the status of 'country' foods consumed mainly in rural areas by farmers who grow their own. The experiment with 'village centres' (des villages centres), launched by the government, is a response to the food deficit and, also prompted by the desire to reach self-sufficiency in food by the year 2000. Under what conditions one attains self-sufficiency in food would be lesson No.4.

There is no hope of economic development with an excessive bureaucracy. Government should offer more responsibilities to those who run enterprises, administrations and business. To reduce the influence of bureaucracy would be lesson No.5.

It does not make much sense to seek economic progress without looking into the possibilities of allocating a large share of benefits, opportunities and income to the rural masses. So far, there has been no attempt on the part of the State to shift the distribution of income. Hence, the disjunction between the political class and the rural masses is going up. Launching a policy of reforms would, of course, be counter to the interests of the ruling class. To shift and redistribute income in order to improve the standard of living of rural masses would be lesson No.6.

With these lessons in mind, there is every reason to be optimistic, as the Congo is not a hopeless case and there are grounds for believing that there is still hope. This would not be the best of all possible worlds; but it would certainly be better than the one we have now.

The Congo can improve its economic and social situations through more efficient officers and with the requisite good will to open to the West and Asian countries. Foreign investment, for instance, over a given period, could help maintain a respectable level of economic growth, but the Congo's bloody colonial experience still makes the country's leadership less enthusiastic about any significant foreign presence.

A period of more than two decades is too short to achieve development but, with a little imagination, progress can be made. The country's future is dependent mainly on the ability of its leaders to reconcile ideology and pragmatism. Also, this country needs a period of at least thirty years of political stability to enable it to implement progress through a development policy. Otherwise it will be 'l'éternel commencement'.

The Other Side of Things: Transition to Socialism

Much has been said about Socialism since the creation of the Congolese Labour Party in 1969. Contradictions have emerged among the revolutionary forces about the passage from pre-capitalist society to Socialism. The problem of transition has a long and chequered history. Two arguments can be distinguished; First, as 'left Communist' N. Osinsky (V. Obelensky) pointed out, the civil war is inseparably linked with a decisive liquidation of private property, the introduction of the Socialist system, and the direct transition to Communism. Second, as Lenin had mentioned at the seventh extraordinary congress of the Bolshevik party; 'We have only just taken the first steps towards shaking off capitalism altogether and beginning the transition to Socialism. We do not know and we cannot know how many stages of transition to Socialism there will be'.[1] Lenin's argument seems reasonable as the transition in itself was related to many factors, which could sometimes accelerate, sometimes slow down the process. Lenin's initial policy for Russia was to try to develop a similar pattern of co-operation with private cartels. This is not to say that transition to Socialism was given up.

By the early 1970s, Ngouabi clarified the situation in the context of the Congo. He raised a relevant question: 'At what stage is our revolution now?' He added, 'our revolution is at the stage of national, democratic and people's revolution'. His followers, especially those who belonged to the M22 group, thought the time had come to move to Socialism. The party was split. This undermined the unity of the Party – the question still remains: to what extent should the Congo move from one step to another?

Today, as Sassou Nguesso has finally accepted I.M.F. supervision of the country's structural adjustment programme (S.A.P.), he is facing several criticisms from the Congolese Labour Party members. In the eyes of many he is selling the State to the capitalist world.

My point of view is that Sassou Nguesso's approval of the I.M.F.'s programme and his privatization programme represents a strategic approach to the transition to Socialism. All measures which have been taken – improvement of performances and reduction of expenditure under the S.A.P. (Structural Adjustment Programme) will facilitate in the long term the welfare of the people. As the economic impact of the Soviet Union on the rest of the world is negligible to speed up development, it is realistic for the Congo for a given period to co-operate with the Western countries and the international organisations. After all, the Soviet Union (at least since Gorbachev came to power) is taking distance from its ideology in economic issues.

We were very conscious of the problem raised by the structural adjustment programme (S.A.P.). For instance, the United Nations Economics for Africa has reached this conclusion: 'The deterioration in the overall economic situation in Africa has continued unabated in spite of impressive efforts at structural adjustment'.

Unlike the World Bank's more optimistic analysis, Africa can have adjustment with growth if its governments implement reforms and donors provide additional resources. [2]

Interdependence

So far, scholars in the field of international economics continue to see the relationship between the North and South in terms of dependence. This is to say that economic links between the developed and the developing countries function at the expense of the latter group. The debate in this question is far from being closed; but on what criteria could one judge 'independence'? Is an independent economy one which is self-reliant, growth being generated from within the domestic market rather than by external demand? In his interesting analysis, Bhagwati has distinguished two types of ideology. The 'benign neglect' which is related to the model of *laissez-faire*.

The idea is, roughly speaking, that the multinational corporations in the developing countries contribute to increase their income, diffuse technology and harness their domestic savings. The opposite of this is 'malign neglect' which sees international trade as a means to perpetuate the role of developing countries as producers of primary products.

More radical than the 'malign neglect' ideology are the conceptions of Marxists and new-left writings with regard to the international economy. According to them, foreign aid is seen as a natural extension of the imperialist designs on the poor nations aimed at creating dependence. [3]

All ideas have a point. However, dependency theory was criticised by a number of writers, especially Warren. Referring to dependency theory as 'nationalist mythology', he argues that:

1. Dependency theory was static in that, although in some versions it recognized the possibility of dynamic development, only the forms of dependency changed, not the situation or condition of dependency itself.

2. The centre-periphery model was taken as given – political independence, nationalism and industrialization in a number of key L.D.C.s were not given their due weight.

3. Direct foreign investment (D.F.I) via trans-national corporations could not be assumed to command political (or even economic) power to host L.D.C. countries.

The dependency perspective seriously underestimated the bargaining power of the L.D.C. state, and a strong state could increasingly integrate trans-national investments into its priorities.

According to Warren, the concept of dependence has always been imprecise. Such significance as it has relates almost entirely to political control of one society by another. Since national economies are becoming increasingly interdependent, the meaning of dependence is even more elusive, not to say mystical. [4]

Without denying a 'third worldist' ideology which sees the poor L.D.C.s as being exploited by the rich developed capitalist economies, the capitalist world which perpetuates unequal exchange, it seems to us more realistic to encourage the developing countries to co-operate with the developed ones.

The theory of breaking down (rupture) with the North seems an illusion. The economies of the developing countries are too weak to allow them to sustain their development by themselves. Interdependence between the developed and the developing countries will make it easier for the latter group to achieve a success in economics. In the case of the Congo, this interdependence will be the starting point of the restoration of the economy and would facilitate the transition to Socialism.

Is Congo a Socialist State?

Quite often students and colleagues asked me, when I was delivering my seminar at the African Studies Centre of the University of Cambridge, 'What is the content of Socialism in the Congo?' This is not easy to answer. As I indicated in the previous chapters, the Congo's Socialism is exceptional. The first point to note here is that from the later 1960s until the later 1970s, there was an increasing role of Marxist ideology and an increasing involvement of the state in the management of the Congolese economy, Congolese Socialism possesses some attributes of a legitimate Socialist order: Nationalization (of the means of production, a working-class ideology). In addition, it possesses other higher Socialist ideals: the welfare of the masses, democracy and authentic consciousness. So far, many human services are provided by the state and all citizens with appropriate qualifications are entitled to free higher education.

In the 1970s, jobs were increased in the areas of education, health, social services, and public administration. Evidence suggests that the state provides 80 per cent of jobs.

With Ngouabi's rise to power, the Revolution was betrayed by an usurping bureaucratic caste.

The meaning of Congolese Socialism has been recently clouded by economic factors. The Congolese economy has been dependent on the state of the world economy. It has developed ties with western companies. The fact that the Congo has developed ties with Western countries for economic aid and today has adopted the IMF structural adjustment programme, reveals that the country is combining Ideology and Pragmatism. To this extent it is clear that Congolese Socialism resembles most developed Eastern countries in principles reflecting Marxist societies. When coupled with economic realities, the Congo leaves aside Marxist ideology. It is this obvious embarrassment created by an experiment of Socialism in Congo.

Notes

1. Roy Medvedev: *The October Revolution* Ed. Constable (London, 1979, p. 131).

2. See Michael Itolman: *African Economics* 'Recovering in financial times' Tuesday May 9th 1989.

3. See Jadish Bhagwati: 'Dependence and interdependence' *Essays in development economics*, Volume 2 (Blackwell, Oxford, 1985, pp. 15–16).

4. See Warren B: *Imperialism: pioneer of capitalism* (NLB and Verso, 1980, p. 182).

Postface

G O TO AFRICA and you will hear the same song, Democracy. The wind
is blowing everywhere and everybody is talking about political change:
Even the largest dictator in Africa is dancing to the same tune of democracy.
Since industrialized countries have linked democracy and aid in Africa, it
is obvious that each African leader is trying to pave the way for democracy.

Does democracy mean freedom, free elections and building up a multi-
party system? For many they have been forbidden to say what they want
and they have been jailed arbitrarily; now the time has come to make
themselves be heard. If democracy can bring freedom and free elections, it
seems to me important to match democracy with prosperity. That is the
real battle of Africa; democracy can work only if individuals are free to
decide what to produce, save and invest. Ideally a country like Congo should
articulate democracy and economy at the same time: unfortunately Africa
in general and the Congo in particular is building up democracy on the
background of tribalism and poor management.

Tribalism and Democracy

Multi-partyism, as everywhere, is spreading like mushrooms in the Congo;
so, anybody could set up his own party. That is the end of the single party.
It is worth saying it is not the first time that the Congo has experimented
with a multi-party system; it was done during independence without success.
The reason behind this was that political leaders had privileged tribes at the
expense of the national interest. Political parties like MSA, PPC and UDDIA
were anchored in each part of the Congo; your political programme doesn't
matter as long as we belong to the same tribes. Are things still the same?

New parties created in the Congo are linked to each area of the Congo:
For instance, UPADS supporters almost all come from le grand Niari
including Bouenza and Lekoumou. At the same time, you will find MCDDI
supporters in the Pool area, RDPS supporters in the Kouilou, RDD in the
Cuvette area. This reality is not subject to discussion and it could compromise political stability. As a president would emerge from one region, it is

clear that the other regions would get together to topple the elected president; excuses would be found to create political troubles.

When political elections take place, many considerations are taken into account to choose a president: above all there are tribal considerations. It is in fact the link that exists in the Congo between politics and tribes which is difficult to break. What are the consequences?

First of all democracy will not bring any prosperity of course; people will not elect someone because they believe they are going to improve living standards. Secondly it seems to me that in the way democracy is being used in the Congo, it will not be possible to provide people with jobs.

Management and Democracy

For many democracy means freedom of expression but we should go beyond this definition: we want democracy because we are expecting people to manage the country very well. In the Congo, with a culture firmly rooted in poor management, democracy will not improve economic performance. People are more and more concerned with how to become efficient in state-owned firms. It is the link between democracy and management which is one of the difficulties encountered by the Congo. Is it possible to combine freedom and management? Indeed we are in need of new ways of thinking about democracy. The values we should pursue are those of being competent and responsible. I see democracy as the way to use your freedom in order to become efficient.

Democracy and Prosperity

Since the Sovereign National Conference in 1991, the move to elect political and economic change was notably widespread. On the political front participants called for multi-party elections and democratic government. On the economic front the Sovereign National Conference insisted on the disaster of the economy caused by the mismanagement of the Congolese Labour Party. Democracy is working in the Congo: legislative and Presidential elections are going to take place; in 1992 citizens will have the right to choose the leaders they want. Now that the excitement of defeating the single party is over, Congolese people are beginning to worry about food and jobs. Nobody is happy, as workers are waiting four months to get a month's salary. It is not enough to give freedom; you have to add this to economic prosperity. At this point, there is no doubt that pressure for higher living standards poses a great threat to democracy in the Congo: while all the leaders in the Congress Palace were calling for freedom, people were asking for economic growth, for prosperity. In my opinion prosperity and political democracy complement one another; free markets and private property function only where people can choose their leaders freely. By the same token, democracy can work only if individuals are free to decide what to produce, save and invest. If there is any link between democracy and market economy, Congo should try to improve its performance on both economic and political fronts at the same time; but this double war is hard to win as one sphere or the other must take priority.

Prospects

No one should forget that Congolese President Sassou Nguesso has been in power nearly twelve years. He presided over the petroleum boom but management was poor. In addition, he was criticized during the National Conference. He lost one part of his power at the expense of Prime Minister André Milongo. Technocrat and apolitical, André Milongo made two mistakes: firstly his cabinet was composed of many ministers from his own area (Pool). Secondly, he didn't do anything to improve the economic situation. Neither Sassou or Milongo will be elected as President. People are fed up with them, while Professor Lissouba is likely to become the next Congolese President. He has an organised and big party which covers almost all parts of the Congo. In addition, he is up to the job and is the only one to make the Congo sort out the mess. Even though problems still remain, I must hold to my prediction.

On the assumption that Lissouba is elected President, he will encounter difficulties in working and implementing his political programme. He will certainly face the challenge of the Congolese Labour Party and MCDDI as well. Congolese Labour Party members will not leave power easily. In my own opinion, the Congolese Labour Party is potentially dangerous to Lissouba's power. PCT will not be happy to see Lissouba succeed where Sassou Nguesso has failed As for Bernard Kolela, MCDDI leader, he would want Lissouba to fail to allow him to take over. So Kolela will conspire with the PCT to topple Lissouba. In these circumstances, Lissouba's projects for society could be undermined by an opportunistic alliance between Sassou Nguesso and Bernard Kolela. Such an outcome would alienate potential foreign investors. Obviously, Congolese people will be the first to pay the price.

The New Axe of the Political Game

It is understood that in the years coming there will be leadership conflict in the north of the Congo. Political leaders like Sassou Nguesso, Yhombi Opangault, Bongho-Nouarra, Bokamba Yangouma, Ganao and Bokilo would like to be considered as the real leaders of the North. As different as they look and sound, all these leaders have something in common: the desire to be president again for some (Sassou and Yhombi) and president for the first time for others. None of them is recognized as the main leader of all parts of the North. So far Yhombi and Sassou are controlling the Continental Cuvette and Yangomna and Bokilo are fighting in order to control the Fluvial Cuvette: while Bongho-Nouarra influence in the West Cuvette is great, Ganao is almost controlling Les Plateaux.

In fact Yhombi is likely to become a respectable leader of the North if he can get Pascal Lissouba on his side and if he can rally Les Plateaux and La Cuvette Ouest.

Another battle will be in the Pool area: two leaders will surely stand for presidency. Prime Minister André Milongo and Bernard Kolela. Because his Party is influential in the Pool area, Kolela is going to become a true leader of Pool. If Kolela maintains his influence in the Pool area, he is likely to go to the second round of presidential elections. Even if he fails to be elected as Congolese president, he will turn himself into the leader of Congolese opposition. This position will be comfortable for him and help him to get organized and fight for the next term. As for André Milongo, he has to have his own political party if he wants to compete with Bernard Kolela. The advantage for Milongo of setting up his own party is to provide him with a framework of ideals to mobilize the voters. To dilute Kolela's influence in Pool, André Milongo must Challenge Kolela. Perhaps Kolela voters will swing to Milongo. In this case, the battle of leadership in the Pool area could be similar to the battle in the North.

Regarding what could have happened in the Niari area, one can safely say that Pascal Lissouba is unanimously considered to be god-like. No one in this area could challenge his leadership for another decade. All three areas of the Grand Niari, including Niari, Bouenza and Lekoumou, are unified and support Pascal Lissouba. Paul Kaya might have been economically competent, but he is not regarded as a true leader in the grand Niari. Above all, he has no political party.

Political Instability

If Lissouba is president, he will run the Congo with a political coalition: this situation will lead to instability as one party will make tactical alliances with another party to undermine Lissouba's project for society. Congo's Constitution doesn't give the President full powers to run the country in the way it should be. The only way for Lissouba to implement his programme and to avoid instability is to control the National Assembly; whether Lissouba's party UPADS make alliance with other parties to consolidate its majority or UPADS wins outright majority from elections. The first possibility requires bargaining including ministers' portfolios. The second one would be useful for Lissouba because he would be able to implement his programme. Do Congolese people understand this?

From Totalitarianism Rule to Democracy

So far Congolese people find the transition from totalitarian rule to democracy rocky. It is difficult to establish a democratic society if there is not a tradition to sustain it: in the past, presidents have been overthrown in the Congo by coup. The kind of multi-party system that is at the heart of Western-style representative democracy was not tolerated. Freedom of expression was banned. Today the struggle for revolutionary Marxist society is being replaced by a more complex and often divisive aim. The first task might be to devolve decision-making power to the local collectives, to put an end to authoritarian methods. Last but not least, what kind of state structure is needed in the Congo? Because of a low understanding of democratic rule in the Congo, if a president does not have full powers, he will not be a driving force for change. A president is elected for five years. I call this period the 'stabilization period', during which the powers of the president are used to ensure that his political programme is being implemented. At the end of this period comes what I call the 'assessment period', during which the majority of people seize the opportunity to consider the president's term. He might have gained confidence or he might have lost it.

As things stand, a strong president who has a free hand to organize government structures, appoint ministers and run by ordonnance is the best model for a country where democratic tradition did not exist before. As it is quite difficult to be a strong president without sliding into totalitarianism, it is fair to give parliament the power to control government activities. While government will appoint, the opposition should keep eyes on a coming dictatorship. This opposition is regarded as an alternative for running the country; England's opposition operates in this manner.

There are certainly those on the political scene who advocate taking power by force. In the situation where the opposition and government do not agree, which leads to personal conflicts and at the same time a compromise of political stability, there would be a risk of a *putsch* by Congolese armed forces. That is the kind of thing which should be avoided, provided political leaders put national interest above personal interests. Are Congolese leaders mature enough to transcend power for power? This still remains to be seen.

Cambridge, January 1992

Appendix

Table 19: Political Parties and Elections

Year 57 58 59 60 61 62 63 64 65 66 67 68 69 70 71 72 73 74 75 76 77 78 79 80

Date
Founded

1956 Union Démocratique De Défenses des Interêts

1946 Mouvement Socialiste Africain

1946 Parti Progressiste Congolais

Mouvement National de la Révolution   Parti Congolais du travail

Independence August 1960	Coup August 1963	Coup August 1968	Constitutional Referendum June 1973	Coup February 1979 General Election & Constitutional Referendum July 1979

Table 20: Annual Instability Events: Independence Through 1975 – Congo

Year	61	62	63	64	65	66	67	68	69	70	71	72	73	74	75
elite instability															
Assassinations															
Plots					I	2	I		I	I	I		2		
Attempted *Coup d'Etat*									I	I	I		I		
Coup d'Etat				I				I							
cabinet instability															
New members	6	2		7	5	3				12	9	4	7		
Resignations & Dismissals,	2		3	5	5				11	9	6	7	1		
Maximum in Year			12	16	16	10	14	11	11	15	15	13	13	12	

Sources: Donald George Morrison: *Black Africa. A comparative Handbook* 2nd Ed. (MacMillan Press Limited, London, 1983).

Table 21: Heads of State (Post Independence)

Name	Dates in Office	Age (1982)	Ethnicity	Education	Former Occupation
1 Abbe Fulbert Youlou (President)	1960–1963	died 1972 at age 55	Kongo (Lari)	Seminary in Akono (Fr. Cameroon)	Catholic Priest
2 Alphonse Massemba-Debat (President)	1963–1968	executed 1977 age 56	Kongo (Lari)	University 'training college' for civil service in French Equatorial Africa	Civil Servant
3 Major Marien N'Gouabi (President)	1969–1977	Assassinated in 1977 aged 40	M'bochi (Kuyu)	French Military Academy	Soldier
4 Gen. Joachim Yhombi-Opango (President and Head Comité Militaire du Parti)	1977–1979	43	Mbochi (born in Owando)	St. Cyr (France)	Soldier
5 Col. Denis Sassou Nguesso,	1979– President	39	Mbochi	Secondary School, French Military School	Soldier

Table 22: Administrative Division in the Congo

Regions	Chefs-Lieux	Districts	PCA
Kouilou	Pointe-Noire	Loandjili M'Vouti Madingou-Nzambi Kayes,	Kakamoeka
Niari	Loubomo	Louvakou Kimonko Kibangou Mossendjo Divenie Mayoki	Makabana Londela Kayes Banda Mougoundou Nyanga Mbinda

Lekoumou	Sibiti	Sibiti	
		Komono	
		Bambama	
		Zananga	
Bouenza	Madingou	Madingou	Mabombo
		Boko-Songo	Tsiaki
		Nkayi	Kingoue
		MFouati	
		Loudima	
		Mouyondzi	
Pool	Kinkala	Kinkala	MBandza
		Boko	Ndounga
		Kindamba	Loumo
		NGamaga	Louingui
		Ngabé	Vindza
		Mayama	
Plateaux	Djambala	Djambala	NGo
		Lekana	MPouya
		Gamboma	MBon
		Abala	Makoutipoko
			Ollombo
Cuvette	Owando	Owando	NTokou
		Makoua	Etoumbi
		Kelle	MBama
		Ewo	Ngoko
		Boundji	Tchikapika
		Okoyo	
		Mossaka	
		Loukolela	
		Milhomo	
		Oyo	
Sangha	Ouesso	Ouesso	Pikounda
		Sembé	Ngbala
		Souanké	
Likouala	Impfondo	Impfondo	Liranga
		Epena	Enyelle
		Dongou	Betou

Source: CNSEE, *Annaire Statistique*, 1982

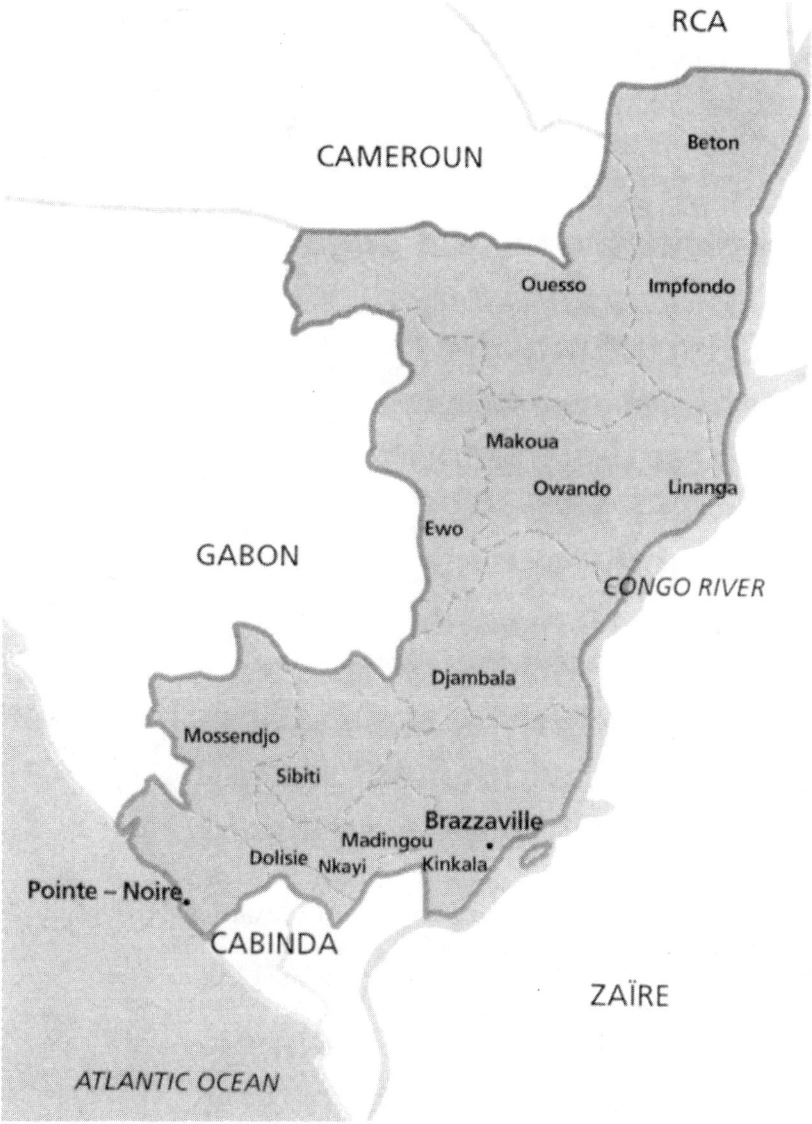
RCA
CAMEROUN
Beton
Ouesso
Impfondo
Makoua
Owando
Linanga
Ewo
GABON
CONGO RIVER
Djambala
Mossendjo
Sibiti
Brazzaville
Madingou
Dolisie
Nkayi
Kinkala
Pointe – Noire
CABINDA
ZAÏRE
ATLANTIC OCEAN

Bibliography

Books

Amin Samir and Catherine Coquery – Vidrovitch: *Histoire economique du Congo 1880–1968*. (Paris, Ed Anthropos, 1969).

Amselle Jean Loup and Emmanuel Gregoire: 'Complicité et conflits entre bourgeoisies d'état et bourgeoisies d'affaires au Mali et au Niger' in *L'état Contemporain* by Emmananuel Terray (Paris, Ed L'Harmattan 1987).

Ballard, John A: 'Four equatorial states. Congo, Gabon, Ubangui-Shari, Chad' in *National unity and regionalism in eight African states* Ed Gwendolen M. Carter Ithaca (NY, Cornell University Press, 1966).

Bhagwati Jadis: 'Dependence and Interdependence' *Essays in development economics*, volume 2 (Oxford, Blackwell, 1985).

Bertrand, Hugues: *Le Congo: formation sociale et mode de dévéloppement économique* (Paris, Ed Maspero, 1975).

Calvocoress, P: *The Congo in world politics since 1945* (London, Longman, 1977).

Ctoce-Spinelli, Michel: *Les enfants de Poto-Poto* (Paris, Ed Bernard Grasset, 1967).

Decalo Samuel: *Coup and Army rule in Africa* (Newhaven and London, Yale University Press, 1976).

Devilliers Cas: *African problems and challenges* (Vallant Publishers, CPTY LTD. 1976).

Duverger Maurice: *Political Parties* (London, 1965).

Eliou Marie: *La formation de la conscience Nationale en République Populaire du Congo* (Paris, Ed Anthropos, 1977).

Gauze Rene: *The Politics of Congo Brazzaville* (Stanford University Press, California, 1973).

Gonidec P. Francois: *African Politics* (The Hague, Ed Martinus Nijhoff, 1981).

Gordon C. Mcdonald: *Area handbook for People's Republic of the Congo Brazzaville* (Washington DC, US Government Printing Office, 1971).

Hilling David: *Congo – physical and social geography in Africa South of the Sahara 1987*, sixteenth edition (England, 1986).

Italiaander Rolf: 'Fulbert Youlou of the Republic of the Congo. A priest becomes President' in *The new leaders of Africa* (Gt Britain, Prentice Hall, Inc 1961).

Lenin: *L'état et la Révolution* (Paris, Ed Seghers 1971).

Marfeje Archie: 'Neo-colonialism, state capitalism or revolution? in *Africa social studies* (London, edited by Peter C. W. Gutking, 1977).

Markovitz I. Leonard: *Power and class in Africa* (United States of America, Prentice Hall, Inc, 1977).

Marx Karl: *Selected Writings* (Oxford, edited by David McEllan, Oxford University Press, 1977).

Nelson: *Ideologies and modern politics* (Great Britain, Edited by Nelson, 1972).

Ngouabi Marien: *Vers la construction d'une société socialiste en Afrique* (Paris, Presence Africaine 1975).

Nguyen Tienhung G: *Agriculture and rural development in the People's Republic of the Congo* (Colorado, Westview Press, 1987).

Obenga Theophile: *La vie de Marien Ngouabi 1938–1977* (Paris, Ed Presence Africaine, 1977).

Radu Michael: 'The Congo' in *Benin, the Congo Burkina Faso* (London, Ed Printer, 1988).

Rey Pierre Philippe: *Colonialisme, Nécolonialisme et transition au capitalisme* Exemple de la 'comilog' du Congo Brazzaville (Paris, Ed Francois Maspero, 1971).

Roy Medvedev: *The October revolution* (London, Ed Constable, 1979). Salvatore Foderaro: *Independent Africa* (Colin Smythe Ltd, England, 1976).

Scarritt James R: *Analyzing political change in Africa* Application of new multi-dimensional framework (Colorado, Westview Press, 1980).

Soret Marcel: *Histoire de Congo Brazzaville* (Paris, Ed Berger-Levrault, 1978).

Thompson Virginia and Adloff Richard: *The Emerging States of French Equatorial Africa* (Stanford, Stanford University Press, 1960).

Periodicals

'Le Congo s'éfforce de redresser une situation économique alarmante' *Le Monde* (27 Août 1985)

'La Révolution Congolaise tiraillée entre Moscou et le MI' *Le Monde* (27 janvier 1987)

'Congo, Un socialisme Africain pas comme les autres' *Le Figaro* (26 decembre 1977)

'New Way in Congo People's Republic' *Africa Communist* (1976) No 59, Fourth Quarter

'Les rapports entre Paris et Brazzaville se dégradent Progressivement' *Le Monde* (19 et 2 janvier 1977)

'Congo, Le Marxizme en question, "Or Noir", "Or Vert"' *Le Monde* (2 janvier 1982)

'Le Congo après seize ans de révolution' *Le Monde*

'Brazzaville enigma' *West Africa* (August 24th 1964)

'Congo, le socialisme à petit pas au plus prés' *Le Monde* (29 Avril 1975)

Bulletin quotidien de L'ACI (17 August 1979)

'Brazzaville. Ten years of Revolution' *West Africa* (August 13th 1973)

'Rise and Fall of Youlou' *West Africa* (August 24th 1963)

'Riots in Brazzaville' *West Africa* (August 17th 1963)

'New Men in Brazzaville' *West Africa* (August 24th 1963)

'Le socialisme Congolais, le point de vue de Pascal Lissouba' *Le Mois en Afrique* (novembre 1966, No 12)

'Congo Brazzaville. Commandant Ngouabi devient chef de L'état' *Le Monde* (2 janvier 1969)

'Ngouabi on Diawara' *West Africa* (May 7th 1973)

'Congo: Anti-Guerilla operation' *West Africa* (March 20th 1973)

'Congo: le spectre de Diawara' *Jeune Afrique* (15 juillet 1972)

'Le Congo de la Radicalisation, une auto critique courageuse' *Le Monde* (23 Mars 1976)

'Congo – le dixième anniversaire de l'arrivée au Pouvoir du General Sassou Nguesso, la Révolution Assagie' *Le Monde* (Dimanche 26–Lundi 27 Janvier 1989)

'Congo. The Revolution goes West' *Africa Confidential* (7th September 1983)

'Congo – Palace coup' *Africa Confidential* (February 28th, 1979)

'Congo – militants take over' *New African* (April, 1979)

'Congo. Denis Sassou – Nguesso takes over' *The African Communist* (1979)

'Congo Ideology is out' *Africa Confidential* (October 1984)

'Congo: Conspiracies Galore' *Africa Confidential* (July 1989)

Articles

Desjeux, Dominique: 'Le Congo est-il situationiste?' *Le Mois en Afrique* (October–November 1980)

Kouka-Kampo: 'Vanguards in the making on the development of revolutionary parties in the socialist oriented countries' *World Marxist Review* (January 1986) Vol. 29 No 1

Lamb David: 'Congo, it can't exist on Marxism' *Los Angeles Times* (July 29th 1977)

Michael Lofchie: 'The Uganda coup – class Action by the Military' *The Journal of Modern African Studies* (January 1972)

N'Gombe Jean Pierre 'Towards a new upsurge of the Revolutionary process' *World Marxist Review* (September 1977) Volume 20, No 9

Ngouabi Marien 'Scientific Socialism in Africa, Congo problems, News and Experiences' *World Marxist Review* (May 1975) No 5 Vol 18

Price Robert M: 'A Theoretical Approach to military rule in new states' Reference Group Theory and the Ghanian case *World politics* (April 1971) Vol 23

Index